DWELL

Learning a Deeper Intimacy with God

Mac and Marya Pier

Movement Day Publishing is the publishing ministry of Movement.org, an organization that catalyzes leaders in more than one hundred cities to see their cities flourish spiritually and socially. Movement.org trains leaders globally to create their own Movement Day Expressions. For more information, visit movement.org.

Dwell © 2025 Mac Pier and Marya Pier

A Movement Day resource published in alliance with Movement.org.

Editor: Charmain Sim
Copyeditor: Christy Distler
Design: Atlas Rosetta

All photos used with permission. All rights reserved.

Cataloging-in-Publication Data is available.
ISBN 979-8-9909854-9-0
979-8-9932692-1-4

Printed in the United States of America.

AN INVITATION TO DWELL
FROM GLOBAL LEADERS

THE MIDDLE EAST

In this powerful and deeply biblical book, Mac and Marya remind us of the central truth of our faith, that God's ultimate desire is to dwell with His people.

Rev. Dr. Jack Serra
President, Bethlehem Bible College
General Secretary, MENA Evangelical Alliance, Jerusalem

Mac and Marya have written a dangerous book that has challenged me to the core. To read the Bible meaningfully over a 90-day cycle is stunning. I'm 65 and up to the challenge. Because I want my best days in the Lord to be before me.

Pastor Ray Galea
Senior Pastor, Fellowship Church, Dubai

This book captures Mac and Marya's story in His Presence and invites us to join them on a 90-day journey—dwelling in God's Presence, placing ourselves in His Redemptive Story.

Sona Kazanjian
Coordinator, Movement Day Middle East, Dubai

AFRICA

Dwell is a life companion to every city gospel leader seeking to find God in the brokenness of our cities. A reminder that "the width of our influence is in proportion to the depth of our intimacy with God."

Afia Darkwa-Amanor
Hub Leader, Movement Ghana, Accra

Dwell is an honest, practical, and beautifully written gift of guidance for our journey of faith.

Sandy Watt
Coordinator, Movement Day Africa Scholars Program, Durban

Dwell is a culmination of decades of equipping leaders to refocus our hearts and minds on renewed intimacy with God. We find fruitfulness from dwelling with Him.

Robert Ntuli
Pastor, Living Stones Agency, Dubai

We have come to know Mac and Marya to be a couple of great balance—grounded and visionary, contemplative and action oriented. *Dwell* reflects this beautifully.

Peter Watt
Lead Pastor, 3C Church
Hub Leader, Movement Day Africa, Durban

ASIA

Dwell explains why Mac has been such an effective catalyst for city movements around the globe—his companionship with his wife Marya and their commitment to dwell with God.

Timothy Wong
Co-organizer, SG500 Asia Cities Forum, Singapore

I have seen firsthand how Mac and Marya's deep love for God's Word and prayer has fueled city gospel movements worldwide. *Dwell* is the overflow of that life.

Jerince Peter
Executive Director, Movement South Asia, Chennai

One of the joys of this past decade has been working with Mac and his wonderful wife Marya. Their heart for the gospel is an inspiration. *Dwell* is an outstanding book.

John Snelgrove
Priscilla and Aquila Ministries, Hong Kong

I am grateful for this book. It is timely, timeless, and tender. May it lead you into stillness. May it awaken your heart. And may it help you to truly dwell in His Presence.

Anton Tarigan
Movement Day Indonesia/Center For Kingdom Partnership, Jakarta

Dwell by Mac and Marya is not your typical Bible study guide. It is a deeply personal, heartfelt testimony of lessons they've learned. It is a special invitation to every Christian.

Philip Chang
Regional Director, Lausanne Southeast Asia, Kuala Lumpur

This book will challenge you to "dwell" and linger in God's presence by the practice of reading and meditating on God's inspired, inerrant, infallible and immutable Word.

Seth Kim
Vice President, Arise Asia
Regional Director, Lausanne East Asia, Hong Kong

The book *A Disruptive Gospel* inspired our Disruptive City Women's movement. I am convinced that *Dwell* will now become my next favorite word and anchor.

Kavitha Emmanuel
Disruptive Woman Movement Catalyst, Chennai

I deeply admire the way Mac and Marya live what they teach. *Dwell* is their gift to leaders everywhere—a simple yet profound invitation to spend time daily in Scripture.

Mark Visvasam
Team Leader, Movement Day Asia, Chennai

BALKANS

Dwell is a powerful guide that invites readers into a deeper, more intimate relationship with God through the twin disciplines of immersive Scripture and reflective prayer.

Zefjan Nikolla
General Secretary, IFES Albania, Tirana

This book demonstrates that Movement Day stands behind the principle of deep, systematic, and authentic spiritual life.

Giotis Kantartzis
Pastor, First Evangelical Church, Athens

As Christ dwells richly in us, Mac and Marya's refreshing and reflective approach awakens a desire to pursue these beautiful spiritual disciplines that have shaped their lives.

Johnathan Macris
President, Hellenic Ministries, Athens

LATIN AMERICA

Mac and Marya's ministry transforms cities and leaders alike. Their secret— abiding in Christ—offers a roadmap for faithful and fruitful service that endures.

Leandro Silva
President and Founder, Missao ALEF, Natal

In *Dwell* you will discover God's heart for deeper intimacy with Him through His word. These principles are already being practiced by city leaders globally.

Jose Duran
President, Movimento de Ciudad, Holland, Michigan

Dwell calls us not only to dwell with God, but also to dwell with others, to dwell in our cities, and to live in anticipation of the eternal dwelling in the new heavens and new earth.

Samuel Lima
Movement Day Brazilian Cities, Sao Paulo

NORTH AMERICA

Most of us skim... books, life, God. *Dwell* goes deep—it plumbs the depth of God's Word and our hearts. My good friends, Mac and Marya, go deep. *Dwell* pushes us to get on with it.

Bob Doll
CEO, Crossmark
Board Chair, Movement.org, Princeton

In their book, Mac and Marya guide us in connecting with the Word of God in profound and meaningful ways, helping us to deeply experience God's presence.

DG Elmore
Chairman, Elmore Companies, Bloomington

Dwell is the kind of resource that everyone should have on their bookshelf, but only after they read and use it! Mac and Marya encourage us all to get into these daily disciplines.

Annie McCune
Author, Practicing Hospitality: The Joy and Grace of Loving Strangers, *Atlanta*

Mac and Marya Pier live a life that radiates a deep love for Jesus, This manuscript beautifully reflects the authenticity of their journey rooted in Scripture and service.

Josh Miles
Managing Director, Movement.org, Lexington

Dwell invites us to experience God both wide and deep. Mac's 90-day journey offers the sweeping story of God's work across history, while Marya's contemplative path encourages us to savor His presence in a single passage.

Eric Swanson
City Leader Collective, Boulder

Dwell is a profound gift to the church. Their blend of Scripture, personal journey, and practical guidance invites believers into a deeper intimacy with God that is transformative.

Rev. Ejaz Nabie
Senior Pastor, Faith Assembly, Richmond Hill

Dwell invites us back into the presence of God. It offers insightful reflections that help turn daily routines into mindful practice. Dwell shows you how to place your life.

Rev. Mullery Jean Pierre
Senior Pastor, Beraca Baptist Church, Brooklyn

Dwell is such a beautiful and fresh invitation into the daily exploration of the Living Word of God. You can actually feel the abiding presence of God hovering over every word!

Rev. Gabrielle Beam
Founder, Rise to Read, Bridgeport

The authors embody what it truly means to dwell faithfully in God's presence. In a society that feels chaotic, fractured, and rushed, *Dwell* invites into a word shaped journey.

Rev. Charles Galbraith
Senior Pastor, Alliance Tabernacle Church, Brooklyn

More than a reading plan, *Dwell* is a sacred guide into God's presence. Mac and Marya help us rest, listen, and encounter Christ in ways that renew the heart.

Bishop Joshua Rodriguez
The Cityline Church, Elizabeth, New Jersey

Dwell challenges the reader to a posture of rest in God's presence. The book's insights are profoundly relevant to our times after fifty years of leadership experience.

Bishop RC Hugh Nelson, D. Min.
Senior Pastor, Ebenezer Urban Ministry Center, Brooklyn

Dwell is a powerful guide that leads believers into a deeper intimacy with God through both the discipline of Scripture and the wonder of His Presence.

Dr. Fernando Cabrera
Lead Pastor, New Life Outreach International Church, Bronx

DEDICATION

This book is dedicated to Noah, Layla, Hayley,
Gabriel, Lily, and Zoey.
May you know the God who longs to Dwell in your heart
all the days of your life and forever.

CONTENTS

WHY DWELL

Why This Book?

As a twenty-two-year-old, I attended
InterVarsity's Orientation for New Staff as
one of the newly initiated. It was at Cedar
Campus in the Upper Peninsula of Michigan.
InterVarsity is an eighty-year-old campus
organization that builds communities of
Christian college students to impact their
campus with the gospel. I had previously been
active with InterVarsity as a student and a
chapter president but had no formal theological
training at that time.

One of the orientation speakers was Barbara
Boyd. She had founded Bible and Life, an
InterVarsity program that trained thousands
of students in the disciplines of quiet time
and inductive Bible study. Boyd was one of
the great spiritual mothers for many college
students. Tim Keller was profoundly impacted
by her teaching while an InterVarsity student at
Bucknell.

The orientation took place in July 1981, forty-
four years ago. I remember Boyd's teaching on

the lives of Eli the priest and Samuel the boy (1 Samuel 3) as though it were yesterday. The Lord was calling Samuel by name—the God of the universe speaking to a twelve-year-old child. He disclosed to Samuel the fate of Eli and Eli's family. This family would be put to death and their family line would be extinguished for their blasphemy against the Lord in their sacred roles as priests.

Samuel obeyed the word of the Lord and told Eli everything. The chapter ends by saying, "The LORD was with Samuel as he grew up, and he let none of his words fall to the ground. And Samuel's word came to all Israel" (v. 19). Samuel could speak to all of Israel because God had all of Samuel (1 Samuel 3:19–41).

Boyd applied this truth to the history of InterVarsity. In the early days of the organization, Boyd had worked with several senior colleagues. She shared rather soberly that a few of these colleagues walked away from their faith by the end of their lives. There was a holy hush over the room. We were gripped by the holiness of God and the extraordinary freedom that we have to receive and obey—or disobey—the word of the Lord. Boyd commented that these colleagues did not wake up one day and decide that their faith was not true. It was a slow disengagement with God and His Word over time that resulted in perilous decision-making.

Why this book? I believe that the older we get and the longer we journey with God, the deeper we must go. One of the dangers of a long faith journey is that the familiar can become unfamiliar. When we read Psalm 23:1, for example, the idea of God being our Shepherd can become trite, almost a slogan. We need to instead think deeply and carefully about a Cosmic God who provides in such a way that we will never lack ever. We can become inoculated against the truth and encounters with God unless we commit, with everything in us, to listen and to obey God's Word.

This book is a simple offering, a guide, to experience God in fresh new ways. Marya and I will offer to you some of our learnings from the past fifty years.

READING THE BIBLE TWO WAYS: A GUIDE

This book has two parts. Part 1 is a structured guide to read the Bible chronologically in 90 days. You should do these readings on your own at your own pace. Accompanying each day's reading is my own reflective prayer connected to it. You can do your reading, read my reflection, and then perhaps write your own prayer down. I write my reflections in my iPhone's Notes app. A journal would also work.

In Part 2, Marya will introduce you to *Lectio Divina*, or "divine reading." This will help you to slow down and reflect carefully on a passage of Scripture. It's something we use with leaders from around the world in our Movement Day Scholars Program and at our Pastors' Prayer Summit.

Marya will provide direction for this practice. We suggest doing this once a week privately or with a small group.

OTHER WAYS TO READ THE BIBLE

There are many meaningful ways to read the Bible. The 90-day reading plan in this book is only one such approach. I personally draw deeply from *The Songs of Jesus,* Tim Keller's daily reflection on the Psalms. I also read daily from *A Guide to Prayer for All God's People*, which follows the liturgical calendar beginning with Advent.

During Advent and Lent, I read the writings of Walter Wangerin Jr. in his books *Preparing for Jesus* and *Reliving the Passion.* He is an extraordinary writer. I believe that God draws us to diverse ways of reading the Bible that are consistent with our unique temperament. God has so many mysterious ways He is at work, and I believe that He will draw each of us to Himself both uniquely and collectively.

Reflecting on the life of Samuel in the Bible, I am convinced that the width of our spiritual influence is in proportion to the depth of our intimacy with God. As we look at the extraordinary challenges of cities and nations needing the gospel, the spiritual intimacy of God's people with the God of Revelation is the most important reality that can take place.

THE WORD ON DWELL

In his book, *Dwell: Life with God for the World*, Barry D. Jones writes, "At the heart and center of the staggering story of grace told on the pages of the Bible is the claim that the God of the universe experienced that first rush of oxygen into his lungs when a peasant baby let out his first cry in a stable in Bethlehem two millennia ago. The single greatest difference between Christianity and every theistic religion is succinctly captured in John 1:14, 'The Word became flesh and made his dwelling among us.'"[1]

What makes Christianity, Christianity is this: "God among us." God's ultimate purpose is to dwell among His people. He wants to be present among us and in us.

The word *dwell* is referenced 338 times in the King James Version of the Bible. The first reference is found in Genesis 4:20, and the last is in Revelation 21:3. The theme of *dwell* is quite simply what holds the entirety of the story of creation and consummation together.

Dwell can be defined as:

1.   To live or stay as a permanent resident; reside.

2.   To live or continue in a given condition or state, e.g., to dwell in happiness.

3.   To linger over, emphasize, or ponder in thought, speech, or writing.[2]

Having read the Bible sixty times in the past fifteen years, I am convinced that this theme of *dwell* provides perhaps the most important arc from Genesis to Revelation. This is why we were made. This is what God has been up to from the Garden of Eden right through to the New Jerusalem. God has gone to every possible length to give us the opportunity to both dwell with Him, and to have Him dwell in us. I share five passages that bring this theme to the forefront.

THE FIVE DWELLS

Psalm 23:6—Dwelling in God's Presence Forever

I have read Psalm 23 nearly ten thousand times in the past three decades, and have spent more time studying this passage than any other in my life. I even wrote a twenty-year reflection on Psalm 23 titled *A Disruptive God.*

When I translated Psalm 23 from Hebrew into English, what struck me profoundly was the presence of ten imperfect verbs in the six verses. An imperfect verb is an action that never ends.

In Psalm 23, God is described as One who always provides, always leads us to a place of resting, always restores our souls, always guides us, is always present, always removes our fear, always protects us, always counts us, always prepares a place for us, always pursues us.

In contrast, there are two perfect verbs: *anointed* and *dwell*. God has uniquely anointed each one of us. He also promises us in Psalm 23:6 that we will dwell in the house of the Lord forever.

Everything that happened in David's life and everything that happens in our lives prepares us to dwell with God forever. I believe Psalm 23:6 is the climactic verse of the Old Testament. In God, we are *home. He* is our home. I believe that the more deeply we believe this truth, the greater the risks we will be willing to take for God.[3]

Psalm 133 —Dwelling With God's People in Community

David wrote Psalm 133 to illustrate the power of unity. There are two primary metaphors in this three-verse passage. The first is of the oil flowing down Aaron's beard. Oil in the Old Testament signified God's presence. When we dwell together in unity, we experience the rich presence of God as modeled in the Trinity.

The second image is that of the two mountains—Hermon in the north and Zion in the south. Psalm 133 states that when it rains in Hermon, it gets wet in Zion, signifying that they are connected. In the same way, when God's people are dwelling in unity, they are spiritually connected. This is the intimacy and beauty of unity.

John 1:14—The Word Became Flesh

J. I. Packer summed up this verse beautifully when he wrote, "It is here, in the thing that happened at the first Christmas, that the profoundest and most unfathomable depths of the Christian revelation lie. 'The Word became flesh.' God became man; the divine Son became a Jew; the Almighty appeared on earth as a helpless human baby; unable to do more than lie and stare and wriggle and make noises, needing to be fed and changed and taught to talk like any other child. And there was not illusion or deception in this; the babyhood of the Son of God was a reality. The more you think about it, the more staggering it gets. Nothing in fiction is so fantastic as is this truth of the Incarnation."[4]

It is a gift that Advent is four weeks every year. This gives us a full month to reflect on the wonder, mystery, and miracle of the Incarnation. The delicious truth about the Incarnation is that Jesus came to dwell among us that we might one day dwell with Him forever—even as He has chosen to dwell within our hearts.

Ephesians 3:14–21—That Christ May Dwell in Your Hearts by Faith

In this remarkable epistle, Paul prays for the Ephesian church. This church was birthed out of Paul's historic and courageous visit to this economic center in Asia. From prison, Paul wrote this prayer that the Ephesians would have power.

Power for what, you may ask.

We need power to grasp the fact that Jesus dwells in the heart of the believer. We need power to grasp the full dimensions of God's love in Jesus—its width, breadth, depth, and length. In addition, we need all the saints, the entire body of Christ, to grasp the love of God in Jesus.

We need power to experience Paul's conversion on the road to Damascus where Jesus confronted him with, "Why do you persecute Me?" (Acts 9:4). From that moment, Paul understood that Jesus was so intimately identified with His church that to persecute the church was to persecute Jesus.

The more we comprehend that Jesus dwells in our hearts by faith, the more we will comprehend that we are part of a universal church that spans the globe and reaches back into the millennia.

Revelation 21:3—God's Dwelling Place Is Among His People

Both world history and church history climax with this realization: What God has been striving for since eternity past, when He dreamed up and created the world, was that He would dwell among His people. The one thing we can give God that He can't give Himself is human companionship. He has the companionship of the Trinity, but before creation He did not have human companionship.

When God created galaxies and giraffes, the cosmos and cattle, He climaxed His creation by making us in His image. God, above all else, is a relational being. The Trinity is an eternal community of the Godhead. He wants us to participate, to dwell in this eternal community with Himself.

Ever since The Fall in the Garden of Eden, and the Ancient Promise that God would crush the head of the serpent, God's intent of dwelling among His people has been unfolding and will be culminated in the New Jerusalem.

The final metaphor for the church is a city in which all of God's people dwell together with Him forever. The four-thousand-year arc from Abraham to John's Revelation climaxes here with God dwelling with His people in the New Jerusalem. The Garden has given way to the Celestial City.

The goal and hope of this simple book is to guide you, the reader, into an ever-deepening encounter with the God who dreamed you up, who created you, who invited you into His eternal story, and who promises to dwell with you and in you forever.

PART 1:

THE BIBLE
IN 90 DAYS

MAC PIER

WHY 90 DAYS?

I first heard about this discipline in 1983, when Marya and I were short-term missionaries with Operation Mobilization in Ranchi, India. We traveled to a state the size of Nebraska with a population of 100 million, where the ratio of Hindus and Muslims to Christians was 100,000:1. Our team met every Friday to pray for three to nine hours.

In the context of this extraordinary experience, I was told about a leader who had made the 90-day Bible-reading plan part of his own spiritual experience. I tucked that idea away in my mind for the next twelve months.

In June 1984, Marya and I moved to New York City to begin our next chapter with InterVarsity, as I became an area director. I was brand new to New York City, hailing from South Dakota, and feeling completely unqualified to lead a team across fifteen campuses. It was not unlike the feeling of overwhelm that we experienced in India, nor the overwhelm Samuel may have felt in the revelation God gave him.

As we were getting settled into New York City, I had some margin and read the Bible through in 90 days. It was powerful and life-giving to read about God's beauty as Creator, Sustainer, Redeemer, and Rescuer. Reading the Bible this way gave me a larger perspective on the supremacy and sufficiency of God for my own immediate context. My main takeaway was that God has always transcended our risk with His provision.

Then life got really demanding really fast. Campuses started in September. Anna, our oldest daughter, was born in December. Marya was working part-time. I put this discipline away for twenty-five years.

In 2010 a new chapter of life and leadership began, and I felt drawn back to the discipline. I was working with Tim Keller and the City to City team to launch Movement Day in New York City. Three weeks later, I attended the Lausanne Congress in Cape Town, South Africa. There I met Bob Doll through an introduction by Keller. The three of us became the "three-legged stool" of minister, marketplace leader, and missionary respectively, advancing the work of Movement Day.

Beginning January of 2010, I decided to read the Bible cover to cover every 90 days, and have continued this discipline ever since. In the early years, I simply read the Bible through without any written reflection. Eventually, I started writing a short journal entry after each section of Scripture in the form of a prayer. My primary objectives were to look for names of God and to reflect on His character.

Reading the Bible every 90 days is not intended to be a deep, inductive form of Bible study. Themes will stand out. God's character and work will be evident. You will read portions of Scripture that are rarely read. Your appreciation for the revelation and harmony of Scripture will grow exponentially. As N. T. Wright has famously written, two things are essentially true about God: God is King, and God speaks.[1]

The primary reason to read the Bible in 90 days is to keep the full sweep of God's character and work in front of us. From creation to consummation, from redemption to mission, we see the scope of God's activity across the millennia.

READING THE BIBLE CHRONOLOGICALLY

We are all people born in a unique place and time. It has been said that the three greatest mysteries are when you were born, where you were born, and to whom you were born. My parents met because of the Korean War in 1952. Dad had enlisted in the Air Force as a musician and played at officer parties at the Shaw Air Force Base in Sumter, South Carolina. It was during this time that he met my mom, a South Carolina local.

My twin sister and I were born in December 1958, thirteen years after the end of World War II and five years after the Korean War. We grew up in rural South Dakota, where my family has owned a bank since 1914. My great-grandfather not only started a bank but also planted a church.

Being born in America has provided tremendous privileges and opportunities. I was introduced to faith in my local Presbyterian church growing up, and have always known freedom of religion. I experienced a full conversion to the person of Jesus as a high school junior in 1976. Being a Christian leader in America has carried with it extraordinary opportunities and responsibilities. To whom much has been given, much is expected (see Luke 12:48).

In the same vein, it is important to think about the Bible chronologically, as it is the story of God working in space and time. God has choreographed the story of the Bible in a way that is relevant historically and immediately, corporately and privately.

Here are some important dates in the development of the biblical story:

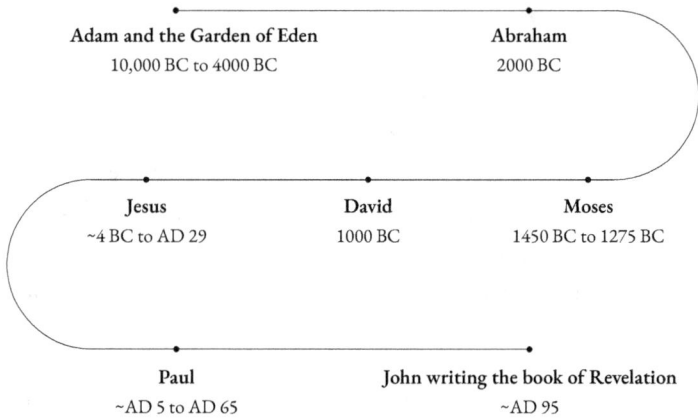

Adam and the Garden of Eden
10,000 BC to 4000 BC

Abraham
2000 BC

Jesus
~4 BC to AD 29

David
1000 BC

Moses
1450 BC to 1275 BC

Paul
~AD 5 to AD 65

John writing the book of Revelation
~AD 95

Another way of thinking about the story of God's redemptive work is provided by Ralph Winter in his article "The Kingdom Strikes Back" for the *Perspectives on the World Christian Movement.* He charts 4,000 years of history into ten 400-year epochs:

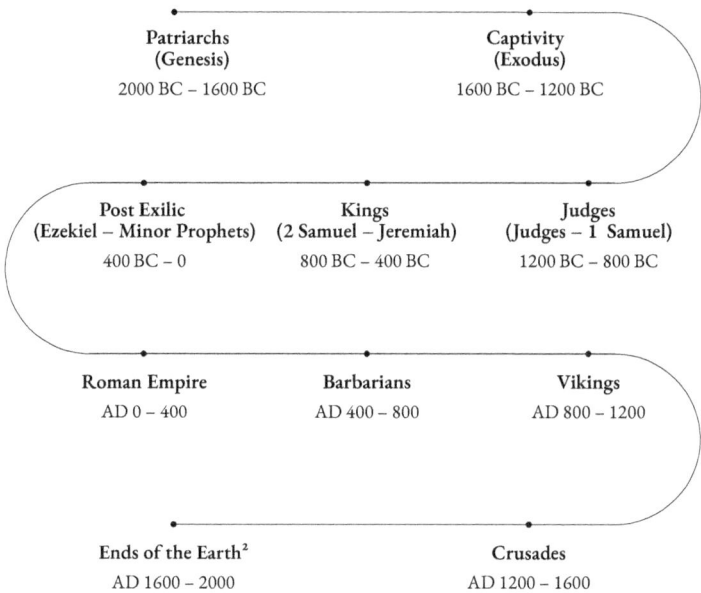

Patriarchs (Genesis) 2000 BC – 1600 BC	Captivity (Exodus) 1600 BC – 1200 BC

Post Exilic (Ezekiel – Minor Prophets) 400 BC – 0	Kings (2 Samuel – Jeremiah) 800 BC – 400 BC	Judges (Judges – 1 Samuel) 1200 BC – 800 BC

Roman Empire AD 0 – 400	Barbarians AD 400 – 800	Vikings AD 800 – 1200

Ends of the Earth[2] AD 1600 – 2000	Crusades AD 1200 – 1600

As we think and read chronologically, we can place ourselves in God's story. As He continues to work out His redemptive plan, we can gain greater insight into how God has worked in the past and how that applies to our present. Ephesians 2:10 reminds us that God has prepared good works for us to do since the foundation of the earth. Understanding the full sweep of Scripture and interpreting our own story through it helps us realize God's assignment for us in the moment.

DISCIPLINED AND
FRUITFUL COLLECTIVELY

What is God's ultimate purpose? In his book *Center Church: Doing Balanced, Gospel-Centered Ministry in Your City*, Tim Keller said that God is not primarily looking for us to be faithful, but to be fruitful.[3] I would add that our fruitfulness will be in proportion to the degree that we understand the reality of God dwelling in us. The reason this devotional is titled *Dwell* is because it speaks to the greatest cosmic mystery of all: *The God of the universe has chosen to come and dwell among us in the person of Jesus. He then chose to come and dwell in the human heart.*

Once we understand this, we will not have a motivational challenge to read the Bible chronologically at least once. Some will want to do this every year. Others will want to pick it up as an ongoing discipline.

Furthermore, I am convinced that the great spiritual movements in church history were always anchored in spiritual disciplines. The Moravians prayed unceasingly for one hundred years from 1727 to 1827. The Franciscans changed Europe because of their disciplines of study, worship, and work. The Clapham Sect ended slavery because their fight for the legal overthrow of slavery was rooted in their hours of daily prayer.

Our spiritual journeys are intensely private yet also important collectively. Just as God dwells in community in the Trinity, we dwell in community with one another. Having shared spiritual disciplines changes not only us but also the world in which we live as we apply God's truth collectively.

THE 90-DAY
READING PLAN

PATRIARCHS
& THE EXODUS

Day 1

Creation, Curse, Covenant

God of Adam—

You created the universe in all of its vast array. From stars to starfish, from galaxies to giraffes, You created everything. Then You created man and woman in Your image, the apex of Creation.

Satan tempted Adam and Eve to eat the forbidden fruit. This was cosmic disobedience resulting in the curse of death. The curse continued in Cain's murder of Abel.

Despite this disobedience and death, You stooped. You stooped to cover Adam's nakedness and Cain's wandering. You went further than stooping, also making Covenantal Promises. You promised to someday bring the True Adam to strike the head of Satan. You gave the rainbow as a Promise never to flood the earth.

In the midst of darkness and death, help me to cling to Your Promises.

Day 2

Job 6—20

The Sufferer

God of Job—

Job's physical suffering was so great that his body was covered with scabs and worms. He had to scrape himself to get any relief.

Job's three friends quickly ran out of empathy and became accusatory. They simplistically associated Job's suffering with his sinning against You. Job's suffering became deeply emotional as well. He was alone.

Job expressed his spiritual suffering. He felt Your absence and silence. One day the True Job would also feel Your absence and silence. You fully entered into my suffering and the suffering of the whole world. You are the True Job.

I confess that many of my days I feel Job's spiritual void. Ground me in the historical reality of Your Suffering for My Salvific Joy.

Day 3

Bitter Complaint

God of Job—

Job was deeply disappointed with You. He accused You of making his life bitter. His questions went unanswered.

Job wondered where You were and why You were so silent. Job wondered why the wicked prosper and the righteous suffer. Job justified himself.

I confess how my own view of You shifts based on personal circumstances. I have never remotely suffered like Job or like so many others across the globe. I complain when my schedule is inconvenienced. I complain when my expectations are unmet.

You mysteriously allow disruption and suffering to do a deeper work in me. You are more concerned about the depth of my empathy than the ease of my life. Give me a fresh confidence in Your mysterious ways as the Cosmic Choreographer of history and my life.

Day 4

I Will

God of Abraham and Job—

You revealed Yourself to both Job and Abraham in personal and powerful ways. To Job, You spoke out of the storm with seventy-six questions. I cannot imagine the God of the universe confronting me with questions about my doubts and criticisms.

Despite Your rebuke to Job, You rebuilt his life. You gave him 140 more years on earth and the joy of seeing four generations.

You gave Abraham the threefold Promise of giving him land, blessing all the nations on the earth through him, and making his name great.

You demonstrated Your determination by stating "I will" six times.

The True Abraham would come one hundred generations later and make it possible for everyone from every nation to be included in Your Promise.

I am the beneficiary of this ancient four-thousand-year-old Promise.

Day 5

Genesis 16—26

Isaac

God of Abraham—

After a twenty-five-year wait, You gave Abraham and Sarah Isaac. They were one hundred and ninety years old respectively. You fulfilled Your Promise to do both the supernatural and the super rational.

Concurrently, You were gracious to Hagar and Ishmael. Though Ishmael was the fruit of Abraham's impatience, You promised to make him into a great nation.

You commanded Abraham to slay Isaac as a test of his faith. Abraham believed You would resurrect Isaac. You disrupted this sacrifice, declaring that Abraham rightly feared You.

This foreshadowed the True Isaac who would come. This time, the knife would not be withheld. This sacrifice would open the door for Abraham's Promise to be fulfilled.

Give me this radical faith, God, to trust You in a super-rational way and to be radically obedient.

Day 6

The Wrestler

God of Jacob—

Jacob lived a contentious life, always deceiving and posturing. He deceived Isaac in his identity, he deceived Esau out of his blessing, and he deceived Laban out of his departure. Laban likewise deceived Jacob for decades.

In the midst of Jacob's character deficit, You kept Your Covenantal Promise to him. You encountered him at Bethel, where he witnessed an angelic staircase.

You encountered him on the eve of his meeting Esau. Jacob thought his days had run out. You wrestled with him all night and disfigured his hip. Jacob the Squirmy Deceiver received a new name. He would be Israel the Wrestler. He could now fully stand on Your Promise.

I too wrestle. I wrestle between a deep confidence in Your Promises and an overwhelming anxiety about current circumstances. I simultaneously rest in You, the True Jacob who wrestles on my behalf for my character formation and my purpose.

Day 7

With Joseph

God of Joseph—

From the slave pit to Potiphar's house, to prison, to the palace—You were with Joseph. For thirteen years Joseph endured imprisonment, yet he endured with his character intact.

You gave Joseph revelation that resulted in the deliverance of global populations through agricultural management. In Your providence, You choreographed the reunion of Joseph with his father and eleven brothers.

You used Joseph to preserve the line of the Messiah. Joseph had become like the future True Joseph who would endure suffering for the rescue of the multitudes.

Give me this prism of understanding in my own suffering.

Day 8

Exodus 1—9

YHWH

God of Moses—

Twenty generations had passed since Joseph, and the Israelites were enslaved in Egypt. You intervened through the birth of Moses. You supernaturally protected him, and he was raised in the courts of Pharaoh.

From his exile in the desert, You called Moses by name. You announced Yourself as YHWH, the God who is:

- Eternally Self Existent
- Initiating Voice
- Unutterably Holy
- Cosmically Concerned
- Great Provider

You used Moses to confront Pharaoh, the most powerful man in the world. You unleashed plagues upon Egypt to demonstrate Your supremacy.

The True Moses will one day come, supernaturally saved at birth to demonstrate Your supremacy in the earth.

Day 9

The Passover

God of Moses—

Your ultimate plague was putting to death the firstborn child in each Egyptian home. The tenth and final plague fully established Your supremacy over the Egyptian gods. This plague sent Israel into its Exodus after four hundred years of slavery.

You had the Israelites institute the Passover. Blood of lambs was placed on the doorposts of each home. The Angel of Death would then "pass over." This has been memorialized for 3,200 years.

The original Passover foreshadowed the True Passover Lamb. He would in fact be sacrificed at the memorial of Passover for our Greater Exodus. Our Greater Exodus has transported us from spiritual death to eternal life. We have been implanted into a new community of former slaves.

I rejoice at Your deliverance.

Day 10

The Intercessor

God of Moses—

Moses spent forty days with You on Mount Sinai. You gave him the law and instructions on the building of the tabernacle. He then came down the mountain to revelry.

Aaron had been persuaded to create the golden calf to represent You and Your deliverance. In Your holy rage, You wanted to destroy the Israelites and begin anew with Moses.

Moses interceded for the nation, appealing on behalf of Your own reputation. Moses then rallied the Levites, who put three thousand to death. You also sent a plague as punishment.

One day You would send the True Moses who would become our Intercessor. Because of His intervention and intercession, I am delivered.

Day 11

Exodus 33—40; Leviticus 1—4

Your Passing Glory

God of Moses—

You rebuked the nation for being stiff-necked. You stated that You would remove Your presence. The removal of Your presence would certainly destroy Your people.

Moses intervened and requested to see Your glory. You were pleased with Moses's request and renewed Your Promise to journey with the nation.

You did not allow Moses to see You face-to-face, for that would kill him. Yet remarkably You permitted Moses to see Your passing glory. Your glory brings Divine Rest.

You then instructed how the tabernacle should be constructed. The tabernacle would provide the space for the nation to encounter Your glory.

Make encountering Your glory my highest aim. Help me to see Your glorious image in my neighbor and in the faces of my city. One day, we will see the glory of the True Moses face-to-face.

Day 12

Holy Offering

God of Moses—

You instituted burnt, fellowship, and grain offerings to express atonement, fellowship, and thanksgiving. As a Holy God, You demonstrated such careful intention to forgive Your people. You reveal the important relationship between sacrifice and forgiveness.

You put Nadab and Abihu to death for their contemptuous treatment of Your holy offerings. Even as priests before You, they were held to a standard of holiness.

You were creating a culture of reverence toward Yourself. You gave detailed instructions on how to live rhythms of forgiveness and gratitude.

Help me to be attentive to Your call to holiness in my life. I give You permission to reveal every shortcoming in my thoughts, behavior, and intentions.

Day 13

Atoning Blood

God of Moses—

In Your instruction on atonement, You ordained that the blood of a creature provides atonement. In the act of sacrifice of an animal's blood, temporary satisfaction of sin was achieved.

Your entire intention is to dwell with Your people, to walk among us. You are a Covenant-Keeping God who promises freedom from sin and slavery. You are a God of Liberation.

You also warn about unfaithfulness. Disobedience will lead to destruction. Your warnings and judgment would unfold in succeeding generations.

Then the True Moses came and offered Himself as the Final Atonement. His blood has forever provided forgiveness for the sins of the world.

I rejoice in my liberation.

Day 14

603,550

God of Moses—

You commanded that a census be taken of fighting men over the age of twenty. You were preparing the nation to go into battle upon entering the Promised Land.

The census is a reminder of Your Promise to Abraham to make him into a great nation. In approximately 430 years, an infertile elderly couple had grown into a great people of millions. Of the millions, 603,550 were of battle-ready age.

You also gave instructions on living life morally, equipping them for life outside the battlefield. You were calling Your people to fully embody Your holiness.

I am so thankful to be counted among the eternal throng of countless followers. You are a Choosing God.

Day 15

Contempt

God of Moses—

The Israelites expressed their contempt for You in their unbelief. Their unbelief expressed itself in the form of complaints.

The Israelites complained about a lack of meat, not believing You could provide for them. Aaron and Miriam complained that You were unfair toward them. The ten spies complained that You would not go with them into Canaan.

The unbelief of the ten, and the subsequent unbelief of the nation, resulted in the judgment of death in the wilderness for a generation.

Their unbelief resulted in a forty-year judgment. This mirrored the forty-day trip the spies had taken to survey Canaan.

You would have destroyed the nation had Moses not interceded.

Give me the audacity of faith to overcome my unbelief. Give me the heart of an intercessor toward those who complain toward me.

Day 16

Quarreling

God of Moses—

Kothan and his fellow Levites confronted Moses. They quarreled with Moses about his leadership. They said that he did not have special leadership status over them.

Moses declared that You would choose between them.

You had the earth swallow these two hundred and fifty Levites and their families. You also sent a plague among the Israelites.

Moses quarreled with the Israelites over a lack of water. In his anger, he failed to follow Your instructions on speaking to the rock rather than striking it. As a consequence, Moses could not enter the Promised Land.

A second plague was sent because of the Israelites' idolatrous relationship with Baal of Peor. This idolatrous relationship resulted in immoral relationships with Midianite women. It was stopped when Phinehas the priest drove a spear through an Israeli-Midianite couple. You honored his zeal.

Ground me afresh in holy zeal for Your Name. Remove from me undisciplined anger that alienates others unnecessarily. Make my zeal proportionate to the depth of Your Holiness.

Day 17

Joshua the Successor

God of Moses—

Moses took the initiative to ask You for a successor. He knew his time was winding down. You appointed Joshua to succeed Moses, and You gave him the spirit of leadership.

You commanded a second census of fighting men over twenty years of age. The number was 601,730. Two plagues had taken a number of lives.

You were preparing the nation for the conquering of Canaan. You were preparing leadership and a division of tribal and family inheritance, ensuring succession for the whole people.

God, help me to understand and respond to the need for holy succession.

Day 18

ALL

God of Moses—

Through Moses You rehearsed the "second law." You repeated the Ten Commandments. You called forth a complete and radical obedience. You were preparing a people to enter a new land.

You pronounced the *Shema*. Everyone was to love You with all their heart, with all their soul, and with all of their strength. You deserve nothing less.

The True Moses would one day come modeling this radical obedience. He would love You with every ounce of His being by loving us with every ounce of His being.

Give me a fresh wonder at this kind of love and sacrifice. May we know and share Your consuming love with all that we have.

Day 19

Moses's Gospel

God of Moses—

Through Moses, You reminded the Israelites that their new land, Your inheritance to the nation, was a gift. Their inheritance was not a reward for their obedience, but was Your judgment on wicked nations.

You commanded the Israelites to remember Your saving acts on their behalf. You commanded the Israelites to obey You. You were dwelling among them, and a Holy God requires a holy people to inhabit.

Moses reminded the nation that he interceded on their behalf for forty days and forty nights without food or water. The nation's survival was a hard-won struggle.

Jesus, You are the True Moses, who is our Gospel. You indwell us and intercede on behalf of us. Make us holy, worthy of Your inhabitation.

Day 20

Death of Moses

God of Moses—

After forty years of leading the nation, Moses dies on Mount Nebo. No other leader in world history knew You face-to-face.

Moses had led a nation out of four hundred years of slavery to the edge of Canaan. He rehearsed Your covenantal faithfulness to Israel. He gave them the choice between fidelity and prosperity, and disobedience and death. You commanded obedience.

You brought Moses to the edge of Canaan, where he died at Mount Nebo. I have seen from Mount Nebo the signs that point toward Jerusalem and the Mediterranean. Moses's death is that great intersection between history and eternity, between Your purposes and our humanity.

You also promised that Israel could dwell in the shadow of the Almighty (see Psalm 91:1).

You are our Covenantal Protector. I dwell with You as You dwell in me.

JUDGES
&
KINGS

Day 21

Be Strong and Courageous

God of Joshua —

You commanded Joshua four times in the opening chapter of his book to be strong and courageous. Joshua's strength and courage would be the antidote to Moses' death.

You performed the Second Exodus, as You caused the Jordan River to stand still while the nation passed through. You called forth Covenantal Consecration through circumcision.

Rahab was full of faith, believing You would come and conquer Canaan. The scarlet thread was the symbol of her faith.

Achan, the heir of the Promise, coveted the sacred belongings. He and his family were stoned then burned. Your holiness is exacting.
The land was distributed tribe by tribe. The Levites received no inheritance as You are their inheritance.

Give me the strength and courage to lead into my Levitical calling. May You be sufficient.

Day 22

Promise Keeper

God of Joshua—

You fulfilled every promise made to the Israelites. You are the Covenantal God. Every tribe received their inheritance.

Joshua commanded obedience to You. He summarized the benefits of obedience and the consequences of disobedience. He had the nation reconsecrate themselves to You.

Joshua died at 110 years of age. The bones of Joseph were brought to his new resting place.

You kept Joshua alive to see the day where every one of Your Promises came true. While a generation perished in the desert, You honored Joshua's obedient faith. He was able to lead Israel into the Second Exodus across the Jordan into Canaan.

Give me the courage to obey You. Help me to fully live in my inheritance in You.

Day 23

Gideon's 300

God of Gideon—

Israel began a downward cycle of disobedience and decline. Over successive generations, the Israelites cried out to You, and You raised up judges to deliver them.

You called Gideon to defeat the Midianites. You stooped to Gideon's doubt by giving him two signs. You then whittled Gideon's army down to 300 who supernaturally defeated the Midianites.

You used a range of judges to deliver Israel, including Deborah, Ehud, and Othniel. As time marched on, the prevailing darkness over the nation deepened.

Deliver me from my doubt, and deliver me and Your church in all of our Helplessness.

Day 24

The Kindness of God

God of Ruth—

The end of Judges and beginning of Ruth are about the harshness of life. Syncretism and idolatry led to a violent civil war, nearly exterminating the Benjaminites.

Naomi's life was devastated by famine and death. She lost her husband and two sons. She intended to return to Bethlehem empty-handed.

Your kindness intervened in the life of Naomi and in the nation through Ruth and then Boaz. Both of these demonstrated a generosity of kindness. Ruth was generous toward Naomi, and Boaz was generous toward Ruth.

Ruth gave birth to Obed, who was the forerunner to a future King. You would provide for a leaderless and defeated nation through the birth of a Son.

Day 25

Samuel

God of Samuel—

After You had closed Hannah's womb, she prayed desperately for a son. Hannah wanted a son; You wanted a leader. Those two wants intersected in Hannah's prayer asking You to remember her, and in her vow to return Samuel to You all the days of his life.

Samuel did not let Your words fall to the ground. He led fearlessly as Israel's prophet and judge. After he prayed, You thundered, allowing Israel to defeat the Philistines.

Samuel anointed Saul as Israel's first king. Israel was rejecting You as their king. It was the beginning of an ill-fated monarchy.

Give me the heart's desire to not allow Your Word to drop to the ground. Give me the courage to match my prayers to a vow.

Day 26

Deliverer King

God of David—

You had Samuel anoint David to succeed Saul. You regretted choosing Saul after a series of disobediences. You chose David, a very young man, to be king of Israel.

You gave David the determination to deliver Israel from the hand of Goliath and the Philistines. With a sling and stone, David triumphed, demonstrating Your superiority over the gods of the Philistines.

For the next decade You would deliver David from Saul. David extolled Your deliverance, Your beauty, and Your salvation.

I declare to You, my Deliverer, that I need Your deliverance afresh.

Day 27

The Rescuer

God of David—

You rescued David from three-thousand-member search parties sent by Saul to kill him. You rescued David and his men from those who kidnapped their families. You rescued David from Absalom. You rescued David from Goliath. At every turn, David saw You as His Rescuer, even in the eleventh hour.

You preserved David's life in accordance with Your Promises. Saul, in an act of spiritual corruption, sought a medium to conjure Samuel. He was told that he would die in battle along with his sons.

You are our Great Rescuer. One day the True David would come and rescue us from eternal death. We owe You our lives, God. I owe You mine.

Day 28

2 Samuel 1—4; 1 Chronicles 1—2;
Psalms 6; 8—10; 14; 16; 19; 21; 121; 123—125; 128—130

King David

God of David—

After Saul's death, David was named king of Judah. After seven years of civil war and intrigue, David consolidated his throne over all Israel.

Abner was a central figure who brought Saul's house to David. He killed Joab's brother, and Joab in turn killed Abner. David killed the Amalekite who killed Saul. An eye for an eye.

Yet, David saw Your gloriousness, Your trustworthiness, and Your beauty. He saw Your long-term faithfulness over the decades. You had fulfilled Your promise of making him king.

I rest and trust in Your faithfulness today, God.

Day 29

1 Chronicles 3—6; Psalms 43—45; 49; 73; 77—78; 84—85; 87

My Portion

God of David—

As David was established as king, he was mindful of You. You were present. You were his portion. Your temple was his dwelling place.

Even as David was king, You are the Eternal King. You superintend the universe. Your promises are fulfilled. Your purposes prevail.

The True David is coming—the One who will be forever present with us, making His Temple inside of us. Your purposes transcend the uneven obedience of Your followers, of me.

I bask in the knowledge and experience of Your presence, God. Be the source of my joy.

Day 30

2 Samuel 5:1—10; 1 Chronicles 7—12;
Psalms 81; 88; 92—93; 102—104

A King in Jerusalem

God of David—

You fully established David as king in Jerusalem. You fully established Jerusalem as the religious capital of the world. You had given David victory over his enemies.

David pronounced You as the God who heals all of our diseases and who forgives all of our sins. How could he say that? He was pointing toward a True David who would one day come, removing our sins as far as the east is from the west (see Psalm 103:12).

I revel in Your kingship and in Your forgiveness. I bless You with every ounce of my being.

Day 31

2 Samuel 5:11—25; 6; 1 Chronicles 13—16;
Psalms 1—2; 15; 22—24; 47; 68; 133; 106—107

The Great King

God of David—

In his kingship, David brought the Ark of the Covenant to Jerusalem. This happened after Uzzah mishandled the Ark and was struck dead. This was a reminder of Your holiness.

As the Ark returned, David led the celebration with great dancing and joy. David declared Your kingship over the whole earth. You are the Great King. You fulfilled Your promise to David through Samuel, that he would be the future king. After a decade of life as a refugee being chased by Saul, You established David.

The psalmists remind us that You are not only the Great King, but You are also the Holy One. You are the Sufficient, Present, and Promise-Keeping God. I trust in You today.

Day 32

2 Samuel 7—9; 1 Chronicles 17—18;
Psalms 25; 29; 33; 36; 39; 89; 96; 100—101; 105; 132

Building David's House

God of David—

In his zeal, David planned to build You a house. You in turn declared that You would build David a house that would last forever. In that house, You would dwell forever.

In David's house You would dwell as the Eternal King. Your Covenantal Promise to David was unconditional. Though David lived out his kingship imperfectly, Your Promise is sure.

How is this possible? Because a future True David would come. He would come as the ultimate Temple. Miraculously and supernaturally, He would make His Temple in us.

For that, we join the whole earth to resound Your glorious praise. To You, the God Who Thunders.

Day 33

2 Samuel 10—12; 1 Chronicles 19—20;
Psalms 20; 50; 53; 60; 65—67; 69—70; 75

Utter Contempt

God of David—

In a moment of extraordinary indiscipline, David caved in to his sexual desires. He completely abused his power over a woman, over a soldier, and over a marriage.

This indiscipline took a life and shattered David's leadership. These acts of adultery, abuse of power, and murder would affect his family and nation for a generation.

You called it utter contempt. There were severe consequences, including the death of the infant son. David knew better. He tried in vain to cover up his behavior.

Yet You forgave David. You did not negate Your Promise to him. We are David. Despite our own foolishness—my own foolishness—You promise forgiveness toward repentant hearts.

Fill my heart and mind afresh with Your holiness even as I swim in Your unrelenting mercy.

Day 34

2 Samuel 13—18;
Psalms 3—4; 12—13; 28; 32; 51; 55; 86; 122

Absalom's Conspiracy

God of David—

Nathan's prophecy came true regarding David's family. Amnon raped Tamar. Absalom killed Amnon. Absalom committed a treasonous coup against his father.

David fled Jerusalem and was cursed by a relative of Saul. It seemed that Your Promise to David regarding an eternal kingship was voided.

Yet You delivered David. You allowed Absalom to receive the counsel that would lead to his own death at the hands of Joab. David regained his kingship but lost a son.

In a great irony, You temporarily lost Your Son that He might gain us as part of His eternal kingship. I rejoice in Your deliverance.

Day 35

2 Samuel 19—23;
Psalms 5; 26; 38; 40—42; 57—58; 61—62; 64

Kingdom Restored

God of David—

After Absalom's death, David returned to Jerusalem. You restored him. Even so, He was humbled and grieved by Absalom's conspiracy.

David saw that despite all the family trauma, You had kept Your Promises. You had surrounded David with loyal mighty men.

David commanded his own soul to rest in the truth of his salvation. You are a saving God in the midst of our daily need for deliverance.

Like David, I live in complex realities. These realities are a mixture of joy and grief, of achievement and setbacks, of loyalty and betrayal.

What sustained David and what sustains me is that You are the Unwavering King, the Rock of Ages. Be my King today.

Day 36

2 Samuel 24; 1 Chronicles 21—25;
Psalms 30; 95; 97—99; 108—110

Awakening the Dawn

God of David—

David made a presumptuous decision to count the fighting men. It
represented a self-confidence in Israel's military might. You responded
by sending a plague.

You lifted the plague by commanding David to build an altar for
sacrifice and worship. You mysteriously use sacrifice, which leads
to deliverance. You are a God that responds to the worship of Your
people.

As David prepared Solomon for succession, he was careful to
strengthen temple worship. David was a radical worshipper.
Worshipping You filled him with joy. In worship, he understood You as
King Eternal. In worship, he awakened the dawn.

Give me this heart of worship during the watches of the night that I
may awaken the dawn.

Day 37

David's Death & Solomon's Enthronement

God of David—

David's life concluded with him preparing for the building of the
temple. He provided organization and resources toward that task. He
gave his very heart for this task.

David also established Solomon as king. After some intrigue with his
son Adonijah and his captain Joab, David declared the choosing of
Solomon. Adonijah and Joab were put to death.

David declared You as the Eternal King. You are completely
trustworthy as a God Who Is Present and Promise-Keeping.

Day 38

Solomon's Revelation

God of Solomon—

You invited Solomon to make any request of You. Solomon then asked for wisdom to govern Your people. You were pleased with Solomon and responded with great promise to prosper him.

You were answering David's prayer of Psalm 72 to establish Solomon as a king whose legacy would endure forever. Psalm 119, the epicenter of the Bible, celebrates You as a Revelatory God.

Solomon wrote Song of Solomon as an allegorical expression of Your affection for Your people. You are not only a Revelatory God; You are a God that reveals His affection for His people.

I bask today in Your revelation and affection.

Day 39

Wisdom at All Costs

God of Solomon—

Having a fear and reverence of You is the beginning of wisdom. You are the Holy and Transcendent God. You command us into a life of judgment and discipline.

You urge us into a life of fidelity. You urge us to pursue understanding at all costs. You warn us of the realities of self-destructive behavior.

Guard my heart and my mind that I may not dishonor You or the sacred relationships in my life. You are the Great God of Wisdom. Help me drink from Your fountain.

Day 40

Temple Building

God of Solomon—

Solomon deployed 153,600 workers in the building of the temple and the palace. King Hiram provided the cedar for these magnificent structures.

It was on Solomon's heart to build a temple where Your Name would dwell. He desired a temple that was worthy of the God of the Universe. For more than a decade, these laborers built the temple.

You are the God of Wisdom and Revelation. You are the Creator God. You are the Compassionate God of the Poor. Fill my heart with a full revelation of Yourself. Help me to worship Jesus, the True and Ultimate Temple.

Day 41

1 Kings 7—8; 2 Chronicles 4—7;
Psalms 134; 136; 146—150

Dwell

God of Solomon—

The temple was finished. The nation was gathered. Solomon prayed his dedicatory prayer—that You would hear the prayers of Your people, that You would heal the land, and that You would forgive their sin.

This dedicatory prayer is the high watermark of Your dwelling with Your people in Your temple. You are a Prayer-Hearing and Promise-Keeping God.

You affirmed Solomon that You had heard his prayer, You would heal the land, and You forgave their sin. You are the Prayer-Initiating God.

The response of Your people? Ecstatic worship. The unimaginable happened. You came to dwell among Your people. Even more unimaginable, You now dwell in Your people as the Temple God.

Day 42

Solomon's Promise & Peril

God of Solomon—

You spoke to Solomon at the twenty-year mark of his kingship. The temple and palace had been completed. The nation had had three generations of Davidic and Solomonic rule.

You promised Solomon that continued faithfulness would be rewarded with a never-ending dynasty. You warned him that disobedience would result in ruin and expulsion.

Solomon wrote of the meaninglessness of life. After twenty years, his behavior became self-destructive. He no longer operated with the fear of Your holiness that You deserve.

Grip my heart afresh today with Your transcendence and holiness. Give me the daily and momentary discipline to live in awe of You.

Day 43

1 Kings 10—14; 2 Chronicles 9;
Ecclesiastes 7—12; Proverbs 30—31

Apostasy & Civil War

God of Solomon—

Solomon was completely undisciplined in relationship to his many wives. He clung to their gods and committed idolatry. You tore the kingdom away from his son Rehoboam.

Rehoboam failed to listen to his elders. He was so harsh with his subjects that eleven of the twelve tribes abandoned his kingship.

Israel and Judah then went to civil war. The nation began a long, slow downward spiral that resulted in exile. You would judge the personal and national apostasy.

May we remember individually and collectively that You are our Creator. Help me to live with nobility. You are our Holy God.

PROPHETS
&
EXILE

Day 44

Fire & Rain

God of Elijah—

After Ahab became king of Israel, You sent Elijah to confront his idolatry. Elijah declared a drought for three years. You supernaturally provided for Elijah via a raven and then a widow.

Elijah created a showdown with the four hundred and fifty prophets of Baal on Mount Carmel. He challenged them to call down fire on their altar and sacrifice. After hours of their unsuccessful chanting, Elijah then called on You. You responded immediately and overwhelmingly with a Consuming Fire.

Then the rains came, ending the three-year drought. Exhausted, Elijah ran for his life from Jezebel. You met him, providing rest and food. You stooped to meet Elijah in his need.

One day the True Elijah would provide the Ultimate Rest. Give me Elijah's ferocity of faith.

Day 45

Ahab's Death

God of Elijah—

Ahab and Jezebel continued to do evil and commit idolatry. The zenith of their evil was to falsely accuse Naboth, have him murdered, and steal his vineyard. You vowed that dogs would lick their blood, and their entire clan would perish.

Ahab was killed in battle. Dogs did lick his blood. Your judgment began on Ahab's household. You kept Your word.

All of Israel's kings after Solomon were evil. The nation was hurtling toward exile. Your forbearance was running out. You will punish evil.

Help me protect my own heart from evil tendencies. Give me the discipline of self-awareness.

Day 46

Chariot of Fire

God of Elisha—

Elijah was taken to heaven by a chariot of fire. Elisha received a double portion of Elijah's spirit, becoming the dominant spiritual voice in Israel.

Elisha performed supernatural exploits—raising the dead, healing the leper, and defeating adversarial kings. Elisha was the forerunner to the True Elisha who would perform supernatural miracles to authenticate His identity.

Jezebel was put to death. All of Ahab's family was put to death in fulfillment of prophecy. Even in the midst of a declining nation, Your Word was fulfilled.

I pray for demonstrations of Your power in our world and in my culture. May my life authenticate Your power and reality.

Day 47

2 Kings 14—15; 2 Chronicles 25—26; Isaiah 1—4; Jonah 1—4

Concerned

God of Jonah—

In the context of a dying kingdom, You took action. You called Jonah as a missionary to Nineveh, a violent and corrupt city.

You called Jonah to transcend his ethnocentrism against the Ninevites. He ran the other way. He would rather be disobedient than see the Ninevites spared Your wrath.

You stooped to intervene in Jonah's actions through the whale and the worm. You stooped to teach Jonah that You are a God of Great Concern.

Jesus would come as the True Jonah who would leave heaven to warn us of a coming wrath. Lord Jesus, You absorbed that wrath that we could become sons and daughters.

Day 48

Isaiah 5—12; Amos 1—9; 2 Chronicles 27

Zeal

God of Isaiah—

The prophet Amos condemned the injustices in Israel, bringing the nation to the brink of exile. The nation's idolatry had risen before You, resulting in Your condemnation. You commanded that justice flow like a river.

The prophet Isaiah declared that You would give a sign, an Emmanuel coming into the world. This sign would be God among us as Wonderful Counselor, Everlasting Father, Prince of Peace, Mighty God.

Why would You do this? Because You are a Zealous God. You will stop at nothing to fulfill Your grander purposes. You will come thundering and roaring.

Give me the powers of apprehension to see You demonstrating Your zeal in this day. Give me the spirit of zeal to achieve Your purposes.

Day 49

2 Kings 16—17; 2 Chronicles 28; Isaiah 13—22; Micah 1—7

From Bethlehem

God of Micah—

Even as You declared Your judgment of the nations and of Israel, You promised an Ancient Ruler. One was coming who would be both a Deliverer and a Savior.

Israel was on the brink of exile. It had broken covenant in its idolatrous and unjust practices. You declared what is required of Your people—to do justly, to love mercy, and to walk humbly with You.

Help me to walk in these requirements. Give me the strength to be as zealous toward Your purposes as You are toward me.

Day 50

Out of Bethlehem

God of Hosea—

You commanded Hosea to marry an adulteress. Gomer was a representation of Israel's infidelity. Though Israel was unfaithful, You pursued her with Your unconditional love.

Your love was so great that You prophesied that a True Hosea would come out of Bethlehem as the Ultimate Lover, the Ultimate Pursuer. This True Hosea would be a Savior and a King.

Help me to apprehend Your pursuit of me, of Your church. You are the God of Compassion and Mercy. Help me to pursue You.

Day 51

The Great King

God of Isaiah—

Sennacherib declared himself to be the great king. You responded to his arrogance by putting 185,000 of his soldiers to death. Sennacherib himself was killed at the hands of his own sons.

You were demonstrating and declaring that You are the Great King. You are the Supreme God. You are the God Who Brings Salvation and Joy through rest and repentance.

You are the God of Deliverance. You are the Great King. I exult in my own deliverance and salvation. You have rescued me and rescued Your people from the most difficult of circumstances.

Day 52

2 Kings 18:9—19; Isaiah 40—53; Psalms 46; 80; 135

Maker, King, Servant, Redeemer

God of Isaiah—

You are the Creator and King of the universe. You are also Servant and our Redeemer. You are the Great Sufferer for our salvation.

You are the Choosing God. You chose Israel as Your possession. You have chosen us as Your workmanship. You are the Lord.

Fill my heart and my horizon afresh with Your magnificence. Manifest Yourself to me. Make me like Yourself, entering Your suffering for the world.

Day 53

Anointed Conqueror

God of Isaiah—

Under the reign of Manasseh, Judah was hurtling toward judgment and exile. Blood from injustice filled the street.

Against this backdrop, Isaiah had a vision of Your glory among the nations. Kings brought their tribute foreshadowing the Messianic encounter with the Magi.

Isaiah envisioned a future Messiah that would declare Good News for the poor. You would draw the nations into a house of prayer. Your people will give You no rest until You accomplish Your purposes in all the earth.

This Anointed Conqueror will come and establish a New Jerusalem where infants do not die. Its citizens will live past one hundred years of age. The people will dwell in the land and flourish. Fill our hearts with hope as we see the horizons of Your Promises.

Day 54

2 Kings 22—23; 2 Chronicles 32—35;
Zephaniah 1—3; Nahum 1—3

Josiah

God of Josiah—

You raised Josiah as king of Judah at eight years old. During his thirty-one-year reign, he was a powerful reformer. He rebuilt the temple and instituted the reading of Scripture.

Josiah removed the idolatry of his father Manasseh from the temple. He was zealous for Your Name. Despite all of his reforming ways, Your anger still burned against the evil of Manasseh.

Josiah's successors were evil. You were preparing the nation for exile. You were also judging the Assyrians for their cruelty.

And yet . . . there was the promise of restoration. You are the Trustworthy God who sings over His people. Let me hear Your joy over Your church.

Day 55

Jeremiah 1—17

Appointed

God of Jeremiah—

You knew Jeremiah before You formed him in the womb. You appointed him as a prophet to the nation for forty years. Across four kingships, Jeremiah prophesied the impending destruction of Jerusalem.

The nation had become completely idolatrous. It was depending on other gods and other nations. The nation had aroused Your anger and hatred.

You gave Jeremiah the metaphor of a ruined linen belt. This described the relationship between You and the nation—one of utter uselessness.

Help me to understand my own assignment. Remove from me any useless character flaw and independent spirit. I declare my absolute dependence on You.

Day 56

Fire in My Bones

God of Jeremiah—

In the midst of a dying nation and death threats, Jeremiah prophesied. You gave him the metaphor of a pot waiting to be smashed. The nation would be captured and destroyed.

The nation would experience forty years of exile. Then You would restore Your people and Your nation. You had a plan to prosper Your people. You would give Your people a new heart and a new covenant.

The True Jeremiah would someday come. He would provide a forever home and fulfill a forever covenant. I trust and rest in that truth.

Day 57

Fall of Jerusalem

God of Jeremiah—

King Nebuchadnezzar's army marched to Jerusalem and captured it.
The temple was burned and its articles were removed. A severe famine
settled over the city.

Your words through Jeremiah came true. You judged the nation for its
idolatry. The nation was sent into exile. Your cup of wrath was now
full.

Even in the midst of judgment, You are acknowledged as Savior and
King. You are working out Your sovereign purposes. In the midst of
destruction, You have a plan for restoration.

Do Your restorative work in me today.

Day 58

In Wrath Remember Mercy

God of Habakkuk—

Just as Jerusalem fell, You were preparing to judge the nations. You would judge the Babylonians for their pride and their idolatry. You judged the Philistines into extinction.

You are the Holy One. You stride through the earth delivering judgment on evil. You pierce the head of the wicked with their own spear.

Habakkuk appealed for mercy in the midst of judgment. You are Savior. Though there were no cattle in the stalls or grapes on the vine, Habakkuk trusted You. He knew how to look back at Your ways and to look up in Your transcendence.

We trust in Your holiness, in Your supremacy, and in Your sufficiency. Help me to look back at Your faithfulness and to look up in Your transcendence.

Day 59

Lamentations 1—5; Ezekiel 1—4

390

God of Ezekiel—

You commanded Ezekiel to bear the sin of the nation by lying on his side for 390 days. This represented the number of years of Israel's idolatry.

You commanded Ezekiel to be a watchman for the nation. Ezekiel would speak Your words to the nation. Ezekiel ate the scroll You gave him. Ezekiel would fully ingest Your Word before he spoke it to the nation.

Though the nation was exiled and Jerusalem destroyed, yet Your love and faithfulness still maintained Your inheritance. You promised restoration. A True Ezekiel would come, forever bearing the sins of the nation.

Help me to understand and repent over my personal and our collective national sins.

Day 60

Ezekiel 5—17

Glory Departed

God of Ezekiel—

In Your disgust at the idolatry in the Temple, Your Glory departed. You could no longer maintain Your presence among Your people. You would make Yourself unmistakably known in Your judgment.

You equated Israel to an unfaithful wife. She had trusted in her beauty and courted other lovers. Israel made alliances with other nations rather than trusting You.

You equated Israel to a useless vine. She was unfruitful in representing You to the nations. Israel would need to be radically pruned to bear fruit.

Help me to receive Your pruning, God. I want my life and Your church to bear fruit.

Day 61

Ohola & Oholiba

God of Ezekiel—

You accused the nation of lewdness and prostitution. Ohola and Oholiba were sisters who represented Israel's spiritual adultery. Israel and Judah chased after other nations to protect them. They were spiritually adulterous toward You.

Our personal and national hearts are inclined away from You. We trust our own chariots and political alliances. We trust our careers and personal networks more than we trust You.

Forgive and cleanse me. Forgive and cleanse our global church. We are overmatched in our own moral and financial reserves. You are the Lord.

Day 62

For My Holy Name

God of Ezekiel—

You declared fifty-eight times in Ezekiel's book "then they will know I am the LORD." You made Yourself unmistakably known in Your judgment of the nations including Egypt.

You made Yourself unmistakably known by becoming Israel's Shepherd and by giving everyone a new heart. You promised to return and restore Your people.

You made Yourself unmistakably known by resurrecting a valley of dry bones into an army. This is the penultimate miracle of the Old Testament, pointing to the True Ezekiel who would come and be resurrected before resurrecting all of His followers.

Why? You are absolutely and eternally committed to display Your holy name. I live in and rest in that truth.

Day 63

Temple Glory Restored

God of Ezekiel—

In a complete reversal of Your judgment, Your Glory returned to Israel and to the Temple. In Your providential and sovereign will, You restored Your people.

You restored the Temple itself with great specificity of its architecture. You restored the Levites who administered worship in the Temple. You emphatically stated that You were the inheritance of the Levites.

You restored the tribes and their ancestral inheritance. You provided great specificity to their boundaries. You are the Restorative God.

One day the True Ezekiel would come. He would be the Forever Temple of God. Miraculously and mysteriously, He would make us all His Temple.

I am lost in wonder at Your supernatural ways.

Day 64

Dream Revealer

God of Daniel—

You sovereignly placed Daniel and his friends in places of influence. You gave Daniel revelation regarding the dreams of Nebuchadnezzar and his son Belshazzar. Each revelation pointed toward Your supremacy.

Daniel and his friends overcame death threats. The friends were thrown into a blazing fire and survived. Daniel was put in a lion's den and survived.

You protected them from great danger, allowing them to share Your superiority to the world. You honored their courage, their witness, and their discipline.

You are actively at work today, drawing kings and princes to Yourself. Use my leadership to fulfill Your purposes in these places.

Day 65

Temple Renewal

God of Ezra—

You providentially motivated King Cyrus to allow the Jews to return to Jerusalem. They were given permission to build a new temple.

The remnant met resistance politically under King Artaxerxes. King Darius then gave them permission to resume their work.

Both Ezra and Haggai challenged the Jews to continue to build the Temple. Upon completion, Ezra read the law for the renewing of Your people. He rebuked those men who had intermarried with foreign women, resulting in religious syncretism.

This points to the True Ezra who would come as the fulfillment of Law and Temple. You are always preparing a place for Your people to *Dwell*.

Day 66

Zechariah 1—14; Esther 1—10

King on a Colt

God of Zechariah—

Zechariah prophesied Your triumphant entry into Jerusalem five hundred years before it happened. You are the King of history, choreographing events for Your grander purposes.

You promised full restoration to Your people as You shepherded them. You had a plan for the nations.

You also intervened providentially in the lives of Mordecai and Esther. You raised up an orphan who would become queen. Under Mordecai's influence, Esther saved the Jewish nation from genocide.

Esther's bravery made Zechariah's prophecy possible. Current courage makes future redemption possible. Give me courage.

Day 67

Joy of the Returned

God of Nehemiah—

You stirred Nehemiah's heart to rebuild the gates of Jerusalem and the citizens of the city. You gave him revelation after four months of fasting, weeping, and repentance.

You gave favor with the king to provide Nehemiah all that he needed—personnel, provisions, and political permissions. You gave Nehemiah both courage and strategy to rebuild the wall in fifty-two days.

As important as the wall was to the safety of the city, so was the covenantal identity among Your people. Nehemiah called out usury practices that enslaved Jew to Jew. The Jewish people were to live a lifestyle of joyous worship and dependency.

Fill my heart afresh with joy as the beneficiary of Your Redemptive Story.

MESSIAH
HAS COME

Day 68

Word Made Flesh

Jesus—

After four hundred years of silence, You arrived as the Word Made Flesh. You were born as the fulfillment of Ancient Promises. You came as a first-century Jew born in the Roman Empire.

Word from the beginning, Your arrival into the world was met with great joy expressed by the angels. You tied Your ancestry to four women who were a Gentile, two prostitutes, and an adulteress—You came into the world identifying with sinners.

Your coming shocked Zechariah, Joseph, Mary, and the shepherds. The angel commanded each one to not be afraid.

Knowing You came into the world, may I live and lead unafraid and rest content in You.

Day 69

Isaiah 40

Jesus—

John the Baptist came preaching repentance, baptizing many. He understood himself to be the fulfillment of Isaiah 40. He was preparing the way for You, the Messiah.

When John saw You, he declared You the Lamb of God. You had John baptize You, and the Father spoke from the heavens that You were His Son. You then fought temptation with the commands of Deuteronomy.

Your baptism and temptation in the desert were to identify Yourself with us.

Isaiah 61 was fulfilled in Your coming. You came to preach Good News to the poor, and to transform the world through Your chosen disciples.

Thank you for choosing me. Help me to follow You with the same zeal You pursued me with.

Day 70

Lord of the Sabbath

Jesus—

You demonstrated Your authority in word and deed. You purposefully chose to heal on the Sabbath to reorient the Jewish nation to a correct understanding of Yourself.

You gave the Sabbath as a gift to Your people to demonstrate trust and worship. You healed the broken as a gift. You are the Sabbath Incarnate, the One in whom we find our rest.

You call forth a radical counterculture of forgiveness and anxious-free living. We need not worry. You will honor every effort to ask, seek, and knock.

Help me to ask, see, and knock.

Day 71

Matthew 8:1–13; 11; 12:22–50; 13; Luke 7–8

Great Faith

Jesus—

You commend the faith of the centurion for believing in Your authority to heal. You marveled at the faith of a Gentile. He understood how You act despite the great cultural differences. You are the Great God Who Acts on our faith.

You used Your authority to raise the dead and to heal the demonic. John the Baptist questioned, and You authenticated Your identity to him by Your authority to heal.

You are the Power of God come to disrupt the broken world we live in. Demonstrate Your power today in my life and in my world. Give me this great faith to trust You to do the supernatural. There are billions of unreached people in the world who need a globe full of followers of Jesus with great faith.

Day 72

12

Jesus—

You demonstrated both Your authority and Your attentiveness in the lives of two women. One woman had been bleeding for twelve years. She touched the hem of Your garment, and her bleeding stopped.

The other woman was a twelve-year-old girl whom You raised from the dead. You even delayed Your arrival to her by giving attention to the bleeding woman.

In each case, You not only performed the supernatural; You did so with great personal attention. You are both the all-powerful and all-present God.

Be present to me today in the painful longsuffering spaces of my own life.

Day 73

Matthew 15—18; Mark 7—9; Luke 9:18—62; John 7—8

Confession, Prediction, Transfiguration

Jesus—

You gave Peter revelation of Your Messiahship. This was an incredibly important moment in Your discipling of the Twelve. Everything would now focus on Your mission to Jerusalem.

You predicted Your death and then Your resurrection. Though the disciples did not comprehend, You were preparing them for that universe-altering moment.

Then the Transfiguration happened. You appeared with Moses and Elijah. In Your life, death, and resurrection You fulfill all the Law and the Prophets.

Grow my heart to apprehend the enormity of these truths. You are the All-Powerful God, come to alter the universe in Your Redemptive Plan.

Day 74

Prodigal God

Jesus—

You came giving sight to the blind and healing the crippled. You demonstrated Your authority over the physical and spiritual realms. You are the Prodigal God doing this with such generosity.

You are prodigal in Your initiative, seeking the lost. You are prodigal in Your sacrifice, laying down Your life as the Good Shepherd. You are prodigal in Your joy, inviting us to celebrate finding that which is lost.

Help me to live and lead prodigally. I want to be a generous and joyful person.

Day 75

I AM THE RESURRECTION

Jesus—

On Your march toward Jerusalem, You predicted Your death a third time. You taught and You healed. Then You announced the trip to see Lazarus.

Lazarus had died. You purposed to travel to Bethany to raise him from the dead. You spoke truth to Martha. You empathized with Mary through Your tears. You proclaimed, "I am the Resurrection and the Life" (John 11:25).

You then commanded Lazarus to come forth. He came out bound hand and foot in his grave clothes. You commanded those around him to release him from the grave clothes.

By raising Lazarus from the dead, You set in motion the resolve of the religious leaders to have You crucified. You were ensuring Your own Crucifixion and Resurrection.

I joy in the knowledge of Your Resurrection, which holds the Promise of my own.

Day 76

Triumphal Entry

Jesus—

In fulfillment of Zechariah 9 and Psalm 118, You came triumphantly into Jerusalem. You came as a King on a colt. You arrived to the shouts of "Hosanna!"

The response was correct, but the understanding was not. The crowd had no idea You would become a Crucified King. You were coming in both salvation and judgment. You came in shouts of exclamation and in tears of sorrow.

The cosmic event of Your Incarnation was nigh. You would glorify Your Father. Your Father affirmed Your obedience.

Give me power to acclaim Your Kingship.

Day 77

Anointed. Betrayed. Arrested. Denied.

Jesus—

The hour had come. You rebuked the religious leaders with seven woes, and predicted the destruction of the temple and the nation. There is a coming apocalypse.

Mary recognized Your coming Passion and anointed You in an act of worship. Judas was possessed by Satan and misguided zealotry, choosing to betray You.

Your betrayal led to Your arrest. You predicted Peter's denial, which came to fruition. You were abandoned and alone, forsaken by God and Your disciples.

Yet, You orchestrated it all for the world, for me.

Day 78

Matthew 27; Mark 15; Luke 22—23; John 13—19

Crucified King

Jesus—

Events had crescendo-ed. The arrest, the trial, the false accusations, the verdict, and now the Crucifixion. You endured every form of suffering—physical, emotional, psychological, and spiritual.

In every dimension of the Crucifixion—the whipping, the tormenting, the spitting, the mocking—there was an identification of suffering with everyone for all time. You had to die, and You had to die the way You died.

Then it was finished. You died fully surrendered to Your Father's will. There was the centurion's confession and Joseph's courage. Already, You were working transformationally in their lives.

Work transformationally anew in my life.

Day 79

Matthew 28; Mark 16; Luke 24; John 20—21; Acts 1—6

Resurrected

Jesus—

You were raised from the dead. You put death to death! You fulfilled Your Promise to be resurrected on the third day.

Your forbearance with Your disciples was extraordinary. After being denied and abandoned, You forgave and empowered Your people. You stooped to the doubt and unbelief by revealing Yourself. You are the Lord.

Your resurrection completely transformed Your followers. Peter the Denier became Peter the Pentecost Preacher. You brought Your followers to a place of unity, boldness, and power.

Breathe on me with Your power of resurrection today.

AGE OF THE
CHURCH

Day 80

A Road-to-Damascus Vision

Jesus—

After the stoning of Stephen, deadly persecution was unleashed on the church. At the epicenter of it was Saul.

On the road to Damascus, You knocked Saul off his horse with Your universe-altering revelation. He experienced an explosion of truth in his mind and heart. You were the fulfillment of Temple and Torah.

To Ananias, You disclosed Saul was Your chosen instrument to preach to the Gentiles and their kings. Saul had a date with Rome.

Barnabas emerged as the most important post-ascension figure of the church. He advocated for, enlisted, mentored, and was companion to Saul. He empowered the greatest evangelist in church history.

Your church is both suffering and multiplying among the Gentiles. Give me a larger understanding of how Your mission is forcefully expanding globally.

Day 81

Acts 15—16; Galatians 1—6; James 1—5

Europe

Jesus—

Paul heard the call from Macedonia, which led him to Philippi in Europe. You opened the heart of Lydia the merchant to receive the Gospel. You added a jailer and a slave girl to the early church.

The church was radically inclusive, with the Gentiles being reached. You were communicating that we were all now one. We have been crucified with You, sharing in Your sufferings.

Paul set forth a new ethic of life in the Spirit, producing love, joy, peace, patience, goodness, gentleness, faithfulness, kindness, and self-control.

Fill me with Your Spirit afresh.

Day 82

Brother Sosthenes

Jesus—

Paul in his fearlessness preached in Thessaloniki, Athens, Corinth, and Ephesus. The Gospel was being established in Greece and Turkey.

In Corinth, one of the converts was Sosthenes. He was a synagogue ruler who was beaten by a Corinthian mob. He became a believer through Paul's influence and a brother in the Corinthian church.

In Athens, Paul appealed to his audience's culture of intellectual thought. In Ephesus, he taught in the town hall of Tyrannus. Paul also performed supernatural acts of healing.

Despite the persecution and fragility of the church, You sustained the boldness of its leaders. Give me fresh boldness.

Day 83

Immovable

Jesus—

Paul challenged the Corinthians to be immovable. Their determination was to be rooted in their confidence in the Resurrection. In the midst of their external and internal challenges as a church, they had grounds for their confidence.

Paul also appealed for an ethic of unconditional love. The kind of love that Paul called for is self-sacrificing and rooted in a culture of forgiveness. Love keeps no record of wrongs.

Because the Resurrection is true, we can love radically and generously. The magnitude of our love will be in proportion to our confidence in the Resurrection.

Root me more deeply in this confidence.

Day 84

Though He Was Rich

Jesus—

The Gospel of God is a story of You emptying Yourself. Though You were rich, You became poor. You became poor to reconcile us to God.

You are the New Covenant. You came to fulfill the Old Covenant and to give Your people a new heart. You demonstrate Your power by stooping to meet us in our great need.

You are the Resurrected God. You authenticate Your claim to be God. Help me to grasp this Resurrection Life in You.

Day 85

Inseparable

Jesus—

Paul built a case for Your love that is both infinite for us and inseparable from us. This love is rooted in the Abrahamic Promise of a righteous faith. This love is a gift that opens the door to eternal life.

The dimensions of this love are so unimaginably great that while we were yet sinners, You died for us. This love is so present that neither death nor life, height nor depth, angels nor demons can separate us from it.

This love is sufficient for the salvation of every Israelite and every Gentile. This love extends from the arrival of Adam to the Consummation of Eternity.

Give me the capacity and competency to fully dwell in all of the dimensions of this love.

Day 86

Rome

Jesus—

Paul reached Rome in fulfillment of his assignment to preach to the Gentiles and their kings. You protected him and providentially provided for him after his capture in Jerusalem. You stood by him and assured him that he would indeed preach in Rome.

From prison, Paul wrote to the Colossians about Your supremacy. Your supremacy is seen in Creation, is seen in Redemption, and is seen in the sustaining of the universe.

Paul wrote to Philemon about Onesimus, the runaway slave who had become a brother. Paul wrote of our sonship in You, the Son of God.

I revel in my sonship today.

Day 87

Ephesians 1—6; Philippians 1—4; Titus 1—3; 1 Timothy 1—6

Chosen

Jesus—

You chose us before the foundation of the world. You saved us by Your finished work on the Cross. You sealed us by the work of Your Spirit for eternity. You dwell in our hearts, King of the Ages.

You chose to be humiliated by Your death on the Cross as a criminal. Now You are exalted to the highest place as Prince and Savior. May Your determination be my determination to fully apprehend why You have taken hold of me.

You are the Immortal, Invisible God. You are Merciful Savior, King of the Universe, Pursuing God. Give my mind and heart the ability to apprehend You.

Day 88

Melchizedek Forever

Jesus—

You are our Great High Priest in the order of Melchizedek. You are the Lamb of God slain for us. You are our Great Intercessor. You who sustains the universe sustain us through Your prayers.

You invite us to worship You in awe. We are in concert with myriads of angels encircling Your throne in worship. You fill us with inexpressible joy. You are the goal of our lives and of eternity.

Fill my heart afresh today with this revelation of Your cosmic reality. You have entered my heart by faith even as You fill the whole universe with Your presence. Joy unspeakable.

Day 89

2 Timothy 1—4; 2 Peter 1—3; 1—3 John; Jude

Persevering Joy

Jesus—

You admonish us through the apostles to persevere. We are to persevere through hardships. We are to persevere over time to see our maturity. We are to persevere in fidelity to the Gospel.

What gives us the strength to persevere? It is Your gift of joy to us. What is this joy? It is You, the Incarnate God who has been felt, touched, and experienced. You are Our Joy.

Immerse me afresh in this joy today. Help me to shed any despondency resulting from discouragement or slowness of heart. May Your indwelling presence be my sufficiency today.

Day 90

Final Dwelling: The Lamb & The New Jerusalem

Jesus—

The Bible and history climax with the Ultimate Dwelling. You are seen as the Lamb of God dwelling with Your people in the New Jerusalem. The final metaphor for the church is a city.

John referred to You twenty-eight times as the Lamb. You are the Lamb of History. You rule kings and nations.

You are the Lamb of Judgment. You finally and fully destroy Satan, the Ancient Enemy. He finally receives his just judgment, being thrown forever into the abyss.

You are the Lamb of Salvation. You were slain before the foundation of the world. You purchased us by Your blood for God.

You are the Lamb of Worship. You are surrounded by 100 million angels. They never stop singing the thrice holy chorus given to Isaiah.

You are the Lamb Who Dwells with His People. What was promised by David, and experienced by John, will be our eternal home. You have come to dwell with us, among us, and in us forever.

PART 2:

52 WEEKS OF
LECTIO DIVINA

MARYA PIER

DWELL IN
LECTIO DIVINA

"The righteous will inherit the land
and dwell in it forever."
PSALM 37:29

"I have indeed built a magnificent
temple for you, a place for you to
dwell forever."
1 KINGS 8:13

Dwell primarily means to live or reside in a place.
A dwelling is a house, an apartment, or another
place of residence. Those of us who follow Jesus
know that this earth is our temporary home,
and we are merely passing through. Our eternal,
permanent home is in heaven with God. To
live on earth as citizens of heaven, we need to
dwell in God's Word so that we can keep our
perspective. We want to be so comfortable in
God's Word and His presence that we are not
only able to live on earth well, but also prepare
to dwell in our eternal home later.

There are many ways to have a quiet time,
or devotions. In my years as a believer, I have
followed many guides, devotional books,
one-year and six-month Bible-reading plans,
and inductive Bible studies. Like many, I have

struggled to get to a quiet place each day for time in God's Word and for listening, worship, and prayer. My desire to go deeper with God led me to study spiritual disciplines, to lead in contemplative experiences at our church for Advent and Lent, and to participate in spiritual and silent retreats. Interestingly, the older I get, the more my need for time in God's Word and in His presence grows.

MY STORY AND TWO QUESTIONS

I am grateful that reading the Bible became a part of my spiritual journey early in life. I saw this modeled in my mother's and grandmother's lives. In high school, I was fortunate to be involved in a youth group that organized a weekly Bible study. In college, I was involved with the InterVarsity Christian Fellowship and learned how to have quiet time, how to study the Bible inductively, and how to navigate my faith and walk with the Lord.

Early in our marriage, Mac and I were fortunate enough to go on a short-term mission trip to the city of Ranchi in northern India. It was there, through our experience with Operation Mobilization missionaries and Union of Evangelical Students leaders, that I learned how to pray for an extended time weekly. I witnessed how God changed people's lives and met them in supernatural ways to reveal Himself. I also learned to go deeper in my faith as an Indian couple mentored Mac and me during our ten weeks there.

When we had small children and I wanted to study God's Word in solitude, I went to the Cenacle Convent and Retreat Center, a Catholic retreat center, for twenty-four hours. At the end of one of these

experiences, a nun asked me, **"What did you hear from the Lord?"**
It was such a simple but moving question, and I began to look at my
devotional time as something more than just receiving information
from the Bible.

When my pastor was working on his doctorate, focusing on spiritual
formation, he asked a few of us to walk alongside him in his study. Part
of our assignment was to visit another church for an Ash Wednesday
contemplative service. We then worked on making that a part of our
church's experience during Lent and Advent seasons. This taught us
meaningful ways to draw others into the practice of spiritual disciplines
through music, silence, meditation, art, washing of feet, and prayer.
What I gained personally in preparing these services was life changing.

When I retired from nursing, I sought more formal education in
spiritual formation. At the direction of a couple of sisters in Christ, I
was led to Leadership Transformations' two-year Emmaus program
in formational leadership. It was usually conducted in community
at a retreat, but due to the COVID-19 pandemic, my experience was
online. Even so, I learned from mentors and leaders, through practice,
instruction, and mentoring, what it means to attend more prayerfully
to the presence of God.

One exercise during this program was to ask ourselves, **"What is
the state of your soul?"** John Wesley, the founder of Methodism,
encouraged his followers to ask a similar hard question: "How is it with
your soul?" He believed that addressing our innermost being was a
crucial part of being in right relationship with God, with one another,
and with the church.[1]

Again, a question that stirred my soul to go deeper in my walk with
Jesus.

WHY LECTIO DIVINA

One practice I experienced in my formational leadership program was the practice of *Lectio Divina*. *Lectio Divina* (pronounced *lex-ee-oh div-ee-nuh*) is Latin for "divine reading" or "sacred reading." Some refer to it as contemplative Bible reading, and it is an ancient way of reading the Bible.

Alice Fryling writes in *Seeking God Together,* "*Lectio Divina* is a way of reading the Bible very, very slowly. Usually only a few verses are read at a time. Sometimes one verse is read. . . Reading the Bible in this way requires an openness to God and a willingness to listen to God's Spirit speaking God's Word into our daily lives. In responding to God's Word deep within the inner resources of our hearts, we are following in the tradition of Moses, of the Old Testament. He said to the Israelites: 'The word is very near you; it is in your mouth and in your heart so you may obey it' (Deuteronomy 30:14). It's good for us to remember when Moses said that, almost no one had access to written Scriptures. Informational reading was not an option for the Israelites! Rather, the word of God was *inside* them. *Lectio Divina* is one way to get Scripture inside our hearts, even today."[2]

Whether you are practicing *Lectio Divina* individually or in a group, it's a method of reading, silence, meditation, and prayer that allows us to go deep in a few verses of Scripture. It is not just reading the Word of God, but also allowing God to use it in transforming our hearts and minds.

These are the five steps or movements of *Lectio Divina* as I learned them (some use four or six):

SILENCIO

A period of silence before reading the passage. It is a time of letting go of your personal agenda and surrendering to whatever God wants you to experience as you read.

LECTIO

Read aloud a short passage of Scripture. As you read, listen for the word or phrase that speaks to you. What is the Spirit drawing attention to?

MEDITATIO

Repeat aloud the word or phrase to which you are drawn. Make connections between it and your life. What is God saying by means of this word or phrase?

ORATIO

Now take these thoughts and offer them back to God in prayer, giving thanks, asking for guidance, asking for forgiveness, and resting in God's love. What is God leading you to pray?

CONTEMPLATIO

Move from the activity of prayer to the stillness of contemplation. Simply rest in God's presence. Stay open to God. Listen to God. Remain in peace and silence before God. How is God revealing Himself to you?

(Another way to do this practice is by reading the passage a second time in another version [i.e., MSG, ESV, KJV, NIV, NLT, etc.]. You can repeat steps 2 and 3, reading the same passage in different versions. This often adds depth or opens up another word or phrase that speaks to our heart in a more meaningful way. This works well when doing Lectio Divina *in a group setting.)*

The following pages offer a guide to practicing *Lectio Divina*. There is also an example of my own personal reading using this practice. The remainder of the book offers fifty-two weekly *Lectio Divina* passages that allow you to experience this divine, sacred reading on your own. I encourage you to follow the five steps for each weekly passage, listening to what God is speaking into your heart before reading or praying the reflection offered at the bottom of each page.

Lectio Divina allows us to meditate on God's Word. It offers a practice of reading that can be done weekly alongside our current Bible reading. It could also be done as our main Bible-reading practice, taking a book of the Bible and covering smaller passages each day.

DWELLING IN GOD'S STORY

Mac and I are sharing with you two of the many ways we have read God's Word over the years. Whether reading through the Bible in 90 days, six months, or one year, we see the completeness of God's plan from creation in Genesis to Jesus's revelation of His second coming, final judgment, and establishment of His eternal kingdom.

Reading the Bible is a powerful experience. We first struggle with the repeated unfaithfulness of God's people in the Old Testament, waiting for the Savior of the world to redeem and save as laid out in the four Gospels. Then we see the disciples witness and suffer as the early church is birthed. We learn through John's visions about Jesus's return. God's story culminates in the revelation of a new heaven and earth, of the worship of God on His throne with the Lamb, of the final judgment of evil, and of the emergence of the Holy City, the New Jerusalem. We learn about the establishment of our eternal dwelling place, our home.

Blessed is the one who does not walk in step with the wicked or stand in the way that sinners take or sit in the company of mockers, but whose delight is in the law of the LORD, and who meditates on his law day and night. That person is like a tree planted by streams of water, which yields its fruit in season and whose leaf does not wither—whatever they do prospers.

PSALM 1:1-3

May our delight be in the law of the Lord, and may we meditate on it day and night.

A GUIDE TO LECTIO DIVINA

1. SILENCE (SILENCIO)

Begin by finding a quiet space. Ask the Lord
to remove the distractions and burdens taking
space in your mind. Prepare to listen to the Lord.
Notice the noise, and try to let go of your agenda
and surrender to whatever God wants you to
hear. Sit quietly for three to five minutes. Perhaps
open your hands and release the distractions into
His hands. You may recite this prayer or use it as
an example:

"Lord, reveal any distractions or burdens that
would hinder me from hearing Your voice or
encountering Your presence."

2. READ (LECTIO)

Choose a passage of Scripture, about four to
eight verses, for this time of meditation. Read
the passage slowly. You may want to read it
aloud. Notice any word or phrase or image that
the Holy Spirit is bringing to your attention.
Take note of it and write it down. You may want
to read it a second time in another version. As
you read and listen, take note of any thoughts

or emotions surfacing within you. You may want to use colored pens or pencils to write those words speaking to you now, in this book, a journal, or a notebook.

3. REFLECT (MEDITATIO)

Take time to actively listen and reflect on what you've written down after reading this passage. Repeat aloud the words or phrases to which you are drawn.

4. RESPOND (ORATIO)

Respond by praying back to God what has surfaced during this time. This may be a call to be more Christlike, a lament, a confession over a sin that has surfaced, or thanks for an attribute or character of God revealed. It may also be something to act on in life or a connection to a personal situation. See this as an opportunity to respond to God as I did with the nun who asked me, "What did you hear from the Lord?"

5. REST (CONTEMPLATIO)

Move from the activity of prayer to the stillness of resting. Take a moment, breathe deeply, and simply rest in God's presence. Remember His affirmation and unconditional love for you. Remain in peace and silence before God. Rest in knowing you've been in His presence and heard from our Lord. Take with you one of the words or phrases revealed to you in this sacred reading experience.

MY EXAMPLE OF LECTIO DIVINA

Passage: Matthew 11:25–30

1. SILENCE (SILENCIO)

I find a place without distractions or interruptions where I can be alone. I close my eyes and open my hands in a position of receiving and readiness.

> *Lord, I pray today that I can meet with You in Your Word in this quiet place. Please remove the worries and distractions of my life as I prepare to hear from You. I'm letting go, in this moment, of all that entangles my mind. Quiet my mind, let me be still.*

I take some deep breaths and wait in silence for a few minutes.

2. READ (LECTIO)

> *At that time Jesus said, "I praise you, Father, Lord of heaven and earth, because you have hidden these things from the wise and learned, and revealed them to little children. Yes, Father, for this is what you were pleased to do.*

"All things have been committed to me by my Father. No one knows the Son except the Father, and no one knows the Father except the Son and those to whom the Son chooses to reveal him.

"Come to me, all you who are weary and burdened, and I will give you rest. Take my yoke upon you and learn from me, for I am gentle and humble in heart, and you will find rest for your souls. For my yoke is easy and my burden is light." (Matthew 11:25–30)

I notice words and phrases:

- Father, Lord of heaven and earth
- Hidden these things from the wise
- Revealed them to little children
- Father (repeated several times)
- Knows the Son (the Father)
- Knows the Father (the Son)

- Son chooses to reveal Him
- Come to me
- Weary and burdened
- Rest
- Gentle and humble in heart
- Rest for souls
- Burden is light

I often re-read the passage in another version:

> *Abruptly Jesus broke into prayer: "Thank you, Father, Lord of heaven and earth. You've concealed your ways from sophisticates and know-it-alls, but spelled them out clearly to ordinary people. Yes, Father, that's the way you like to work."*

> *Jesus resumed talking to the people, but now tenderly. "The Father has given me all these things to do and say. This is a unique Father-Son operation, coming out of Father and Son intimacies and knowledge. No one knows the Son the way the Father does, nor the Father the way the Son does. But I'm not keeping it to myself; I'm ready to go over it line by line with anyone willing to listen.*

> *"Are you tired? Worn out? Burned out on religion? Come to me. Get away with me and you'll recover your life. I'll show you how to take a real rest. Walk with me and work with me—watch how I do it. Learn the unforced rhythms of grace. I won't lay anything heavy or ill-fitting on you. Keep company with me and you'll learn to live freely and lightly." (Matthew 11:25–30 MSG)*

Again I notice words and phrases:

- Spelled them out clearly to the ordinary
- Unique Father-Son operation
- Intimacies and knowledge
- Anyone willing to listen
- Get away with Me
- Recover your life
- How to take a real rest

- Walk with Me
- Work with Me
- Watch Me
- Keep company with Me
- Learn unforced rhythms of grace
- Learn to live freely and lightly

I recognize that even though this is a familiar passage of Scripture, I'm seeing some things for the first time. Jesus is thanking His Father for revealing things clearly to children and to the ordinary. I see the intimate and unique relationship of the Father and the Son. I see Jesus's desire to reveal to anyone willing to listen. I see Jesus with His arms wide open, saying, "Come to Me," "Walk with Me and work with Me"—then only will I learn to live freely and lightly.

I'm struck by how much Jesus desires for us to come to Him, how He wants to reveal things clearly to us, how He doesn't want us to be burdened.

3. REFLECT (MEDITATIO)

What does the Lord want me to hear in this moment?

> My Father has been revealed to me by Jesus.
>
> By coming to Jesus, I will find rest for my soul.
>
> I can let go of all the thoughts and worries I have that tire me out.
>
> Jesus wants me to live freely and lightly.

4. RESPOND (ORATIO)

I come to you, Lord, feeling lighter. I am so thankful that You are the Lord of heaven and earth. I am so thankful that You have reminded me of this unique and special relationship of Father and Son. You've shown me that I can come to You and my worries and burdens will be lifted. I spend so much of my day trying to control all things in my life so I don't have to worry, rather than just coming to be with You so I won't be weary and tired. Help me to bring all things to You first. I come to You and I know a rest only You can give, a peace that only You can offer, and I feel lighter. Amen.

5. REST (CONTEMPLATIO)

I take a moment to rest in what I've heard today by meditating on God's Word. I'm walking away from this time with two thoughts: *"Come to Me"* and *"Find rest."*

52 WEEKS OF
LECTIO DIVINA

WINTER/SUMMER

Silence   ❧   Read   ❧   Reflect   ❧   Respond   ❧   Rest

What words or phrases can you take with you from this experience to apply to your life today?

The Revelation makes explicit what is true of all scripture: it originates as God's word spoken and heard, or presented, and seen. The Christian believes that God speaks and that, as a result of that speaking, all things are brought into being: nature and supernature, the stuff of creation and the relationships of the covenant, and, eventually, scripture. God's word brings the cosmos into existence. God's word accomplishes forgiveness. 'For he spoke, and it came to be' (Ps. 33:9). God has the first word, he has the last word, and all the words in between are spoken in a vocabulary and by means of a grammar that are his gifts to us.
—Eugene Peterson[1]

—

WEEK 2

—

Passage: Isaiah 43:1—7

Silence ❧ Read ❧ Reflect ❧ Respond ❧ Rest

What words or phrases can you take with you from this experience to apply to your life today?

O Lord Jesus, your words to your Father were born out of your silence. Lead me into this silence, so that my words may be spoken in your name and thus be fruitful. It is so hard to be silent, silent with my mouth, but even more, silent with my heart. There is so much talking going on within me. It seems that I am always involved in inner debates with myself, my friends, my enemies my supporters, my opponents, my colleagues and my rivals. But this inner debate reveals how far my heart is from you. If I were simply to rest at your feet and realize that I belong to you and you alone, I would easily stop arguing with all the real and imagined people around me. . . . I know that in the silence of my heart you will speak to me and show me your love. Give me, O Lord, that silence. Let me be patient and grow slowly into this silence in which I can be with you. Amen.
—Henri Nouwen[2]

Silence   ⌄   Read   ⌄   Reflect   ⌄   Respond   ⌄   Rest

What words or phrases can you take with you from this experience to apply to your life today?

God has chosen me—not merely all people—but me specifically, because in his eyes I am holy and in his heart I am dearly loved. I will live this day with the confidence and courage that comes from knowing that I have been chosen by him to live forever with him.
—James Bryan Smith[3]

Silence ❧ **Read** ❧ **Reflect** ❧ **Respond** ❧ **Rest**

What words or phrases can you take with you from this experience to apply to your life today?

We do not always realize what a radical suggestion it is for us to read to be formed and transformed rather than to gather information. We are information seekers. We love to cover territory. It is not easy for us to stop reading when the heart is touched; we are a people who like to get finished. Lectio offers us a new way to read. Read with a vulnerable heart. Expect to be blessed in the reading. Read as one awake, one waiting for the beloved. Read with reverence.
—Macrina Wiederkehr[4]

Silence   **Read**   **Reflect**   **Respond**   **Rest**

What words or phrases can you take with you from this experience to apply to your life today?

We are naturally reverent beings, but much of our natural reverence has been torn away from us because we have been born into a world that hurries. There is no time to be reverent with the earth or with each other. We are all hurrying into progress. And for all our hurrying we lose sight of our true nature a little more each day. This is precisely why we need to believe in the eye of God hovering over us. We are not alone. There is One with us who wants to give back our reverence. There is One with us who wants to give us back the gift of time. Read the Scriptures, then, with reverence, giving up the lie that you don't have time. Read under the eye of God. Read as one who has nothing but time.
—Macrina Wiederkehr[5]

Silence ❧ Read ❧ Reflect ❧ Respond ❧ Rest

What words or phrases can you take with you from this experience to apply to your life today?

And he passed in front of Moses. (Exodus 34:6)

Behind the veil is God, that God after whom the world, with strange inconsistency, has felt, "if haply they might . . . find him" (Acts 17:27). He has discovered Himself to some extent in nature, but more perfectly in the Incarnation. Now He waits to show Himself in ravishing fullness to the humble of soul and the pure in heart.

The world is perishing for lack of the knowledge of God and the Church is famishing for want of His presence. The instant cure of most of our religious ills would be to enter the Presence in spiritual experience, to become suddenly aware that we are in God and God is in us. This would lift us out of our pitiful narrowness and cause our hearts to be enlarged."
—*A. W. Tozer*[6]

Silence ❧ Read ❧ Reflect ❧ Respond ❧ Rest

What words or phrases can you take with you from this experience to apply to your life today?

One author speaks of an "existential loneliness" that permeates every human spirit, a kind of unnamed pain inside, deep within us, a restlessness, an anxiety, a sense of "all aloneness" that calls out to us. I prefer to name it an "existential ache." It is a persistent longing in us and it happens because we are human. It is as strongly present in us as autumn is present in the cycle of seasons. I believe that this ache is within us because we are composed of both physical and spiritual dimensions. Our body belongs to the earth but our spirit does not. Our final home is not here, although "here" is where we are meant to be transformed by treasuring, reverencing and growing through our human journey. No matter how good the "good earth" is, there is always a part of us that is yearning, longing, quietly crying out for the true homeland where life is no longer difficult or unfair.
—Joyce Rupp[7]

Silence   ❧   Read   ❧   Reflect   ❧   Respond   ❧   Rest

What words or phrases can you take with you from this experience to apply to your life today?

Forty days has come to be an excellent period in which to prepare for the Resurrection of the Lord. Jesus took forty days in the wilderness to fast, to fight the Devil, and to prepare for his ministry. Likewise, Moses spent forty days on Mount Sinai, receiving the Law (which no one finally kept but Jesus himself). In the Old Testament a special meaning was attached to the forty-day period: devout encounter with the Lord. But then that meaning was both acknowledged and superseded in the New Testament by Christ's divine activity—and the Law was superseded by Grace!

Observing Lent is an ancient practice of our Christian Church. Examine yourself for your own deep need of Jesus' grace, understanding the crucifixion as the moment of marvelous love and your salvation, and giving God thanks for a resurrection which promises your own in the end.
—Walter Wangerin Jr.[8]

Silence   ❧   Read   ❧   Reflect   ❧   Respond   ❧   Rest

What words or phrases can you take with you from this experience to apply to your life today?

To hear God call our names awes us. To consider facing such an experience without trembling knees is unthinkable. To stand before the One, the author of all that exists, stretches our imaginations to the breaking point. Then to have that One speak our name transforms and changes life. Jesus, too, heard the voice from heaven saying what he already knew. He was God's beloved. What a wonderful message! To be the child of the Creator. To know one is loved like that transforms and prepares us for anything. Perhaps that is why the Gospels tell us that Jesus left the baptismal service and God's affirming voice to go into the desert to be tempted by Satan. Jesus prevailed because he remembered the voice: he remembered who he was and who was with him.
—Rueben P. Job[9]

Silence   ❧   Read   ❧   Reflect   ❧   Respond   ❧   Rest

What words or phrases can you take with you from this experience to apply to your life today?

(On Mark 15:46, describing the burial of Jesus)

There are two sounds in the dusk: the grinding of stone in stone—and once more the soft sigh, a low, compulsive, wordless sigh. Who is that? Then the door is closed. The deed is done. It is finished.

That sigh was me, Lord.

That weeper is me, the twentieth century me, attending your burial. Your dying is never far away nor long ago, but always as close as my own. I cry for the sorrow of being at your death.

But I cry also in gratitude that you will be at my death, O my Savior—and that, though I can only cry for yours, you rescue me from mine. Amen.
—Walter Wangerin Jr.[10]

Silence   ❧   Read   ❧   Reflect   ❧   Respond   ❧   Rest

What words or phrases can you take with you from this experience to apply to your life today?

One of our deepest human longings is to be in communion with God, whose love is revealed to us and embodied in Christ, who in turn loves each of us to the very core of our being. This is matched by our profound yearning to love and be loved, to live in mutual love with our neighbor, which is actually a reflection of God's love for us. Thus our first calling is to dwell in the love of God.
—Gordon T. Smith[11]

WEEK 12

Silence   ❧   Read   ❧   Reflect   ❧   Respond   ❧   Rest

What words or phrases can you take with you from this experience to apply to your life today?

One year during Holy Week, we had a contemplative service where one of the stations included reading this story of Jesus being anointed at Bethany. Perfume bottles were laid out on the table for a person to spray while meditating on the story. I remember how an overwhelming aroma of perfume had permeated the space by the end of the evening. Much like it must have been in Lazarus's home in Bethany.

We also had a room where we listened to CeCe Winans sing "Alabaster Box." Often these contemplative services leave memories. A song, a scent, or a piece of art we looked upon comes to mind every time we hear or read the passage. Allow God to enter your senses as you read His Word, and add a song or a piece of art to enhance this time.
—Marya Pier

Silence ❦ **Read** ❦ **Reflect** ❦ **Respond** ❦ **Rest**

What words or phrases can you take with you from this experience to apply to your life today?

One bold message in the Book of Job is that you can say anything to God. Throw at him your grief, your anger, your doubt, your bitterness, your betrayal, your disappointment—he can absorb them all. As often as not, spiritual giants of the Bible are shown contending with God. They prefer to go away limping, like Jacob, rather than to shut God out. In this respect, the Bible prefigures a tenet of modern psychology: you can't deny your feelings or make them disappear, so you might as well express them. God can deal with every human response save one. He cannot abide the response I fall back on instinctively: an attempt to ignore him or treat him as though he does not exist. That response never once occurred to Job.
—Philip Yancey[12]

SPRING/AUTUMN

Silence   ❧   Read   ❧   Reflect   ❧   Respond   ❧   Rest

What words or phrases can you take with you from this experience to apply to your life today?

He asked her, "Woman, why are you crying? Who is it you are looking for?" (John 20:15)

The Christian life is not always easy. There are joyful moments of walking with Jesus, but there are also times when nothing makes sense and when your world seems to be crumbling. The world will mock your Lord, and you may grow discouraged. At those times, you need to peer into the empty tomb. It is the abandoned tomb that gives you hope, for it symbolizes the life that is yours from your risen Lord. The empty tomb promises that nothing, not even death itself, can defeat the purposes of your Lord. Are you weeping beside an empty tomb?
—Henry T. Blackaby and Richard Blackaby[13]

Silence ❧ Read ❧ Reflect ❧ Respond ❧ Rest

What words or phrases can you take with you from this experience to apply to your life today?

Without solitude it is virtually impossible to live a spiritual life. Solitude begins with a time and place for God, and him alone. If we really believe not only that God exists but also that he is actively present in our lives—healing, teaching, and guiding—we need to set aside a time and space to give him our undivided attention. Jesus says, "Go to your private room and, when you have shut your door, pray to your Father who is in that secret place" (Matthew 6:6 AMP).
—Henri Nouwen[14]

Silence ❧ Read ❧ Reflect ❧ Respond ❧ Rest

What words or phrases can you take with you from this experience to apply to your life today?

Grant me, O Lord, to know what I ought to know,
to love what I ought to love,
to praise what delights thee most,
to value what is precious in thy sight,
to hate what is offensive to thee.
Do not suffer me to judge according to the sight of my eyes,
nor to pass sentence according to the hearing of the ears of ignorant [people];
but to discern with a true judgment between things visible and spiritual,
and above all, always to inquire what is the good pleasure of thy will.
—Thomas à Kempis[15]

WEEK 17

—

Passage: Romans 11:33—12:2

Silence ❧ Read ❧ Reflect ❧ Respond ❧ Rest

What words or phrases can you take with you from this experience to apply to your life today?

Now, God asks us to lay down our lives on His altar as a living sacrifice. Just as it was in the Old Testament, our sacrifice, once offered, cannot be reclaimed. We belong entirely to Him. We cannot make a partial sacrifice of our lives; our offering must be wholehearted.

Therefore, if you are a Christian, your life is not your own. Rather than dying, however, God asks you to live for Him as a living sacrifice. Every day, you are to offer your life to Him for His service. You do not serve Him in your spare time or with your leftover resources. The way you live your life for God is your offering to Him. Relentlessly pursue holiness so that your offering to God is unblemished and acceptable to Him (Eph. 4:1; Phil. 1:27; 1 Thess. 2:12).
—Henry T. Blackaby and Richard Blackaby[16]

Silence ❧ **Read** ❧ **Reflect** ❧ **Respond** ❧ Rest

What words or phrases can you take with you from this experience to apply to your life today?

The biblical record clearly affirms the fact that God knows us and calls us by name as well. We are not strangers or aliens to God. We are each and all God's beloved. We have as our lover the Creator and Master of all that exists. The One who calls us beloved is also the one who knows us so intimately and well that even the numbers of hairs on our head is known.

To remember who creates us and recreates, who calls us again and again, who knows us completely, and who loves us unconditionally is to be prepared, as Jesus was, for all that is to come. We need to have no fear of today or anxiety about tomorrow. We belong to God who claims us as beloved children and holds us close to the embrace of strength and love. Listen and remember today that God calls your name and be transformed and sustained in all that awaits you.
—Rueben P. Job[17]

Silence ❧ **Read** ❧ **Reflect** ❧ **Respond** ❧ **Rest**

What words or phrases can you take with you from this experience to apply to your life today?

When you feel ready, imagine yourself in the historical setting of the story of Bartimaeus as it unfolds in Mark 10:46–52, or imagine yourself in your own place of need. Read the story slowly, seeing yourself as the person needing something from Christ and calling out to him from the noisy crowd. How do you approach him or try to get his attention? What words do you use? What emotions do you feel?

Imagine that in response to your cry, Jesus turns to you. Now you are face to face with one another. Allow yourself the full realization that you have Jesus' complete attention (because you do!) and hear his question addressed to you: "What do you want me to do for you?"
—Ruth Haley Barton[18]

The first time I read this passage in the Lectio Divina practice, I pictured Jesus asking me this same question. Jesus not only asks but also expects us to bring our requests to Him and to believe that He will answer.
—Marya Pier

Silence ❦ Read ❦ Reflect ❦ Respond ❦ Rest

What words or phrases can you take with you from this experience to apply to your life today?

St. Alphonsus Liguori writes, "For a good confession three things are necessary: an examination of conscience, sorrow, and a determination to avoid sin."

Sorrow is an abhorrence at having committed the sin, a deep regret at having offended the heart of the Father. . . . Sorrow is a way of taking the confession seriously.

Remember the heart of the Father; He is like a shepherd who will risk anything to find that one lost sheep. We do not have to make God willing to forgive. In fact, it is God who is working to make us willing to seek his forgiveness.
—Richard Foster[19]

Silence • Read • Reflect • Respond • Rest

What words or phrases can you take with you from this experience to apply to your life today?

Listen, O Lord, to my prayers. Listen to my desire to be with you, to dwell in your house, and to let my whole being be filled with your presence. But none of this is possible without you. When you are not the one who fills me, I am soon filled with endless thoughts and concerns that divide me and tear me away from you. Even thoughts about you, good spiritual thoughts, can be little more than distractions when you are not their author. Every day I see again that only you can teach me to pray, only you can set my heart at rest, only you can let me dwell in your presence. No book, no idea, no concept or theory will ever bring me close to you unless you yourself are the one who lets these instruments become the way to you. But Lord, let me at least remain open to your initiative; let me wait patiently and attentively for that hour when you will come and break through all the walls I have erected. Teach me, O Lord, to pray. Amen.
—*Henri Nouwen*[20]

Silence   ❧   Read   ❧   Reflect   ❧   Respond   ❧   Rest

What words or phrases can you take with you from this experience to apply to your life today?

[Peter's] problem was allowing the Lord to love him profoundly so that he could reclaim the essential fact that Christ and His love for him were most important to him.

That is why Christ asked him three times, "Do you love Me?"—so that Peter could be sure. He needed to know once and for all that it was not what he did or failed to do that was important, but rather that he was loved, forgiven, and cherished. The experience of Peter's spiritual resurrection took place that morning beside the sea he loved so much. Now he knew he loved Christ most of all and was ready to enact resurrection living by feeding Christ's sheep.
—Lloyd John Ogilvie[21]

JUNE

—

WEEK 23

—

Passage: Psalm 18:30–36

Silence ❧ Read ❧ Reflect ❧ Respond ❧ Rest

What words or phrases can you take with you from this experience to apply to your life today?

At the heart of lectio divina is the acknowledgment that our relationship with God the Father is primarily through a person—the Word—not words written in a book.

—Alice Fryling[22]

WEEK 24

———

Passage: Zephaniah 3:17—20

Silence   ❧   Read   ❧   Reflect   ❧   Respond   ❧   Rest

What words or phrases can you take with you from this experience to apply to your life today?

Living between the two comings of Christ, Christians are to look backward and forward: back to the manger, the cross and the empty tomb . . . forward to their meeting with Christ beyond this world, their personal resurrection, and the joy of being with their Savior in glory forever. New Testament devotion is consistently oriented to this hope. Christ is "our hope" and we serve "the God of hope." Faith itself is defined as "being sure of what we hope for," and Christian commitment is defined as "having fled to take hold of . . . this hope as an anchor for the soul" (1 Timothy 1:1; Romans 15:13; Hebrews 11:1, 6:18–19).
—J. I. Packer[23]

WEEK 25

—

Passage: Colossians 1:9—14

Silence   ❧   **Read**   ❧   **Reflect**   ❧   **Respond**   ❧   **Rest**

What words or phrases can you take with you from this experience to apply to your life today?

I promise you, whatever darkness you face is only temporary. Live with an expectation of present victory. Know without a doubt that you will have complete and total triumph in the brightly shining world to come. I encourage you to practice a trusting gratitude even in present darkness. The Light does still shine brightly, even here.
—Terry A. Smith[24]

WEEK 26

———

Silence　⋎　Read　⋎　Reflect　⋎　Respond　⋎　Rest

What words or phrases can you take with you from this experience to apply to your life today?

In Mac's book A Disruptive God, he explains "not lacking anything" as it appears in Psalm 23:1. The first imperfect verb is lack. In the English we translate it as want. The imperfect verb would indicate that a person or a situation is always lacking, always in perpetual need of something. The entire verse turns on the negative proposition not. *Not lack means that since YHWH (God) is paying attention to us, we will never, ever lack—ever.*

We will never lack because YHWH (God) is faithful to us.
—Mac Pier[25]

SUMMER/WINTER

Silence   ❧   **Read**   ❧   **Reflect**   ❧   **Respond**   ❧   **Rest**

What words or phrases can you take with you from this experience to apply to your life today?

Discipleship cannot be realized without discipline. . . . The discipline of the Christian disciple is not to master anything, but rather to be mastered by the Spirit. True Christian discipline is the human effort to create space in which the Spirit of Christ can transform us into his own image. For most of us it is very hard to spend a useless hour with God. It is hard precisely because by facing God alone we also face our own inner chaos. We come in direct confrontation with our restlessness, anxieties, resentments, unresolved tensions, hidden animosities, and longstanding frustrations. Our spontaneous reaction to all of this is to run away and get busy again, so that we at least can make ourselves believe that things are not as bad as they seem in our solitude.
—Henri Nouwen[26]

Silence ❧ Read ❧ Reflect ❧ Respond ❧ Rest

What words or phrases can you take with you from this experience to apply to your life today?

Note carefully how the Lord healed Elijah's depression. He gave him rest and sleep. The prophet had to be rebuilt physically. Then the Lord fed him with nourishing food. When he was rested and refortified, the Lord asked the shocking question which broke the bind: "What are you doing here, Elijah?" He wanted Elijah to get in touch with what was happening to him. Then the Lord sent outward signs of His power: wind, earthquake, and fire. —

But the assurance of the Lord's present came from within in a still, small voice. Elijah was finally quiet, rested, and ready to hear. His status with the Lord was not dependent on his spectacular feats of victory, but on the Lord's love and acceptance. The same fire which had won the victory on Mount Carmel now burned in his heart. Then he sent Elijah back to work, not in his own strength, but with the Lord's. He gave the prophet a new image of himself, a new task and a new power. Discouragement was turned to a new courage. The Lord will do the same for each of us when we take ourselves and our failures too seriously and forget to take the Lord seriously enough.

The fire of the Lord is not just for the battles of Mount Carmel, but for our burned-out hearts.
—Lloyd John Ogilvie[27]

Silence   ❧   **Read**   ❧   **Reflect**   ❧   **Respond**   ❧   **Rest**

What words or phrases can you take with you from this experience to apply to your life today?

Courage is as contagious as fear. Nehemiah had charisma rooted in a firm trust in God's faithfulness. He was sure of His guidance and His strength for the task. The work on the wall was finished with half of the people building and the other half holding spears night and day against the evening attackers. When the work was finished, Nehemiah's enemies were dismayed. He said, "For they recognized that this work had been accomplished with the help of God." God gives us impossible tasks so that we can show others that with Him nothing is impossible.
—Lloyd John Ogilvie[28]

Silence ❧ **Read** ❧ **Reflect** ❧ **Respond** ❧ **Rest**

What words or phrases can you take with you from this experience to apply to your life today?

Thankfulness is a secret passageway into a room you can't find any other way . . . it allows us to discover the rest of God—those dimensions of God's world, God's presence, God's character that are hidden, always, from the thankless . . . to give thanks, to rend it as Scripture tells us we ought—in all circumstances, for all things, to the glory of God—such thanksgiving becomes a declaration of God's sovereign goodness. . . . Inherent in a life of thanksgiving is an ongoing discovery of God's sufficiency, his generosity, his father affection, his warrior protection.
—Mark Buchanan[29]

Silence ❧ Read ❧ Reflect ❧ Respond ❧ Rest

What words or phrases can you take with you from this experience to
apply to your life today?

*Loneliness is the anxiety of unrelatedness. It is caused by an inability to establish,
develop, and nurture deep, lasting and satisfying relationships with other people.
Most of us do not lack for human contact. We usually have more encounters
with other people than we can handle effectively. Our problem is not in the lack
of opportunity but in our deep sense of unrelatedness with those with whom we do
have contact.*

*A person will always be lonely until he or she discovers a deep relationship with
God. Augustine prayed, "Lord, Thou has created us for Thyself and made our
hearts restless until they rest in Thee." Our loneliness is rooted in the lack of
fellowship with God for which we were created. It is in relationship with Him that
we learn what it is to be loved and accepted as we are.*
—Lloyd John Ogilvie[30]

WEEK 32

Passage: Isaiah 11:1—5

Silence ❧ **Read** ❧ **Reflect** ❧ **Respond** ❧ **Rest**

What words or phrases can you take with you from this experience to apply to your life today?

Thank You, Lord for the gift of Your Holy Spirit. The same "Spirit of the Lord that rested on Him, the Spirit of wisdom and understanding, the Spirit of counsel and of might, the Spirit of the knowledge and fear of the Lord." Help me to receive with an open heart Your Spirit. May I be renewed and refreshed by Your Spirit so that I may witness to all of those You have placed in my life and ministry.

Thank You for Your righteousness and faithfulness. Amen.
—Marya Pier

Silence   ❧   **Read**   ❧   **Reflect**   ❧   **Respond**   ❧   **Rest**

What words or phrases can you take with you from this experience to apply to your life today?

My soul is silent before God.
Being silent really means no longer being able to say anything;
It means feeling as if a strange, loving hand is laid on our lips and tells us to be silent.
Being silent means being blessed in the sight of the One longed for and loved;
It means devoting oneself completely;
it means capitulating to the greater power of the Other, the totally Other;
It means for a moment no longer seeing oneself at all, but seeing only the Other,
Yet it also means waiting, waiting to see if the Other has something to say to us.
—Dietrich Bonhoeffer[31]

WEEK 34

—

Passage: John 17:20—26

Silence ❧ Read ❧ Reflect ❧ Respond ❧ Rest

What words or phrases can you take with you from this experience to apply to your life today?

Jesus comes to a sinner, awakens him from his sleep in sin, converts him, forgives him his sins and makes him His child. Then He takes the weak hand of the sinner and places it in His own strong, nail-pierced hand and says: "Come now, I am going with you all the way and will bring you safe home to heaven. If you ever get into trouble or difficulty, just tell me about it. I will give you, without reproach, everything you need, and more besides, day by day, as long as you live."

My friend, do you not also think that that is what Jesus really meant when He gave us prayer?
—Ole Hallesby[32]

WEEK 35

—

Silence ❧ **Read** ❧ **Reflect** ❧ **Respond** ❧ **Rest**

What words or phrases can you take with you from this experience to apply to your life today?

Jesus stands at the door and knocks. What happens when we open the door? Revelation 4 and 5 answers the question and gives the last word on worship in five parts: worship centers, gathers, reveals, sings, and affirms. First in the vision is a throne: "A throne stood in heaven." A throne centers authority. Worship is centering.

In worship God gathers his people to himself as center. Worship is a meeting at the center so that our lives are centered in God and not lived eccentrically. We worship so that we live in response to and from this center, the living God. Failure to worship consigns us to a life of spasms and jerks, at the mercy of every advertisement, every seduction, every siren. Without worship we live manipulated and manipulating lives. We move in either frightened panic or deluded lethargy as we are, in turn, alarmed by specters and soothed by placebos. If there is no center, there is no circumference. People who do not worship are swept into a vast restlessness, epidemic in the world, with no steady direction and no sustaining purpose.
—Eugene H. Peterson[33]

WEEK 36

—

Passage: Psalm 89:1—8

Silence ❧ Read ❧ Reflect ❧ Respond ❧ Rest

What words or phrases can you take with you from this experience to apply to your life today?

As I go now to face the confusion and allurements
of the world's systems,
help me to separate the precious from the worthless,
that I may be your worthy disciple.
Amen.

—*Rueben P. Job and Norman Shawchuck*[34]

Silence   ❧   Read   ❧   Reflect   ❧   Respond   ❧   Rest

What words or phrases can you take with you from this experience to apply to your life today?

It is disconcerting that there is no biblically straight answer to the straight question, "How long?" Yet, even though no date is ever put on the court calendar, a lively belief in God's judgment continues to be firmly held by millions of Christians. What accounts for this persistent belief among people who continue to live with the unanswered questions? For it is most remarkable that communities of faith, in the face of accumulating and not-yet-avenged injustice, persevere in believing that God is just and will judge. The persistence of the prayer "How long?" issues, apparently, from a deep, unshakable conviction that God will bring an end to injustice, even though he shows no signs of calling the court room to order.

—Eugene H. Peterson[35]

Passage: Revelation 21:22—27

Silence 🌢 **Read** 🌢 **Reflect** 🌢 **Respond** 🌢 **Rest**

What words or phrases can you take with you from this experience to apply to your life today?

It has been said that Charles Wesley's hymns always begin on earth and end in heaven. So it is with John Wesley's theology. He was firmly convinced of the coming day of Christ, which is not yet, but toward which humankind, with the whole creation, is moving. For Wesley, it is not necessary to stress God's ultimate victory; but it was also important to affirm the penultimate reality of God's presence, now experienced as life that is drawn to God in increasingly focused love. The Christian lives with the lively hope that God, who has begun a good thing, will fulfill it in the day of Jesus Christ.
—Thomas Langford[36]

Silence ❧ Read ❧ Reflect ❧ Respond ❧ Rest

What words or phrases can you take with you from this experience to apply to your life today?

When Mac and I visited the Areopagus in Athens in 2018, our friend Tom Mahairas asked Mac to read this at the entrance. I pictured Paul being in that spot more than two centuries ago, saying, "The God who made the world and everything in it is the Lord of heaven and earth and does not live in temples built by human hands. And he is not served by human hands, as if he needed anything. Rather, he himself gives everyone life and breath and everything else" (Acts 17:24–25).

What do I worship? What are the things I spend my time and money and energies doing? Jesus is not served by human hands. He gives me everything I have or will ever need.
—Marya Pier

AUTUMN/SPRING

WEEK 40

Silence   🍂   Read   🍂   Reflect   🍂   Respond   🍂   Rest

What words or phrases can you take with you from this experience to apply to your life today?

Be Thou my wisdom, and Thou my true word
I ever with Thee and Thou with me, Lord
Thou my great Father, and I Thy true son
Thou in me dwelling and I with Thee one.
—Dallán Forgaill, "Be Thou My Vision"

WEEK 41

———

Passage: 1 Corinthians 15:50—58

Silence ❧ Read ❧ Reflect ❧ Respond ❧ Rest

What words or phrases can you take with you from this experience to apply to your life today?

Into each of our minds marches a fiendish procession of fears. What is it for you—sickness, failure, loneliness, a loss of love or a loved one? Whatever comes to mind, it is a manifestation of a deeper fear, the one great fear—the fear of death and dying. And yet, we can't really live until we face our own death. The concern is where we will spend eternity.

Paul gives us the basis of the conquest of the fear of death. Our death as Christians is the beginning of the next phase of our eternal life begun there through a personal relationship with Jesus Christ. Multiply the joy of knowing Christ now a billion times, and we have some idea of what is ahead for us. The sting of death has been removed. We are alive forever!

Death is not a final crescendo. It is the last note of the overture to the opera of life to be played out in heaven.
—Lloyd John Ogilvie[37]

WEEK 42

Silence   ❧   Read   ❧   Reflect   ❧   Respond   ❧   Rest

What words or phrases can you take with you from this experience to apply to your life today?

We look at this Son and see the God who cannot be seen. We look at this Son and see God's original purpose in everything created. For everything, absolutely everything, above and below, visible and invisible, rank after rank after rank of angels—everything got started in him and finds its purpose in him. He was there before any of it came into existence and holds it all together right up to this moment. And when it comes to the church, he organizes and holds it together, like a head does a body. (Colossians 1:15–20 MSG)

WEEK 43

Silence ❧ **Read** ❧ **Reflect** ❧ **Respond** ❧ **Rest**

What words or phrases can you take with you from this experience to apply to your life today?

Your desire for more of God than you have right now, your longing for love, your need for deeper levels of spiritual transformation than you have experienced so far is the truest thing about you. You might think that your woundedness or your sinfulness is the truest thing about you or that your giftedness or your personality type or your job title or your identity as husband or wife, mother or father, somehow defines you. But in reality, it is your desire for God and your capacity to reach for more of God than you have right now that is the deepest essence of who you are. There is a place within each of us that is spiritual in nature, the place where God's Spirit witnesses with our spirit about our truest identity. Here God's Spirit dwells with our spirit, and here our truest desires make themselves known. From this place we cry out to God for deeper union with him and with others.
—Ruth Haley Barton[38]

WEEK 44

Silence ❧ **Read** ❧ **Reflect** ❧ **Respond** ❧ **Rest**

What words or phrases can you take with you from this experience to apply to your life today?

The beginning of Psalm 23 verse 3 is really the end of verse 2—He restores my soul. We saw in verse 2 that He leads us beside quiet waters and green pastures. He disrupts our work and drives us to cease. The result of this is having our souls restored. The word restore in Hebrew is translated turn back, which means to restore and refresh.

I interpret the meaning of turning back as returning to home. We are restored and refreshed to the degree that we return to and abide in God as our home. In John 15, Jesus uses the image of the vine and branches. He is the vine; we are the branches. As we rest and abide in Him, we are restored and refreshed.

Over the years I have found that the greatest challenge of spiritual leadership is not program or provision, it is perspective. When we return to God and are refreshed in Him, we are reoriented to the fact that all is His. He owns everything. He initiates everything. He completes everything. I am refreshed in the reality of the inseparable relationship I have in him.
—Mac Pier[39]

WEEK 45

Passage: Lamentations 3:21—26

Silence   Read   Reflect   Respond   Rest

What words or phrases can you take with you from this experience to apply to your life today?

Hopelessness is profoundly personal. . . . Circumstances, people, ourselves, and our talents are not reliable sources of hope.

What we need is a hope that's more than wishful thinking or blind expectations that everything will work out smoothly. We need a hope that is vibrant in pain, consistent in grief, indefatigable when people break our hearts, unassailable in disappointment, and unflagging in life's pressure. Do you have a hope like that? Is your hope ultimately reliable?

True hope is inadvertent. It does not come from searching for hope. It grows out of two basic convictions: that God is in charge and that He intervenes. This is why a true experience of Christmas gives us lasting hope.

The ground of hope is Christ in the world, but the evidence of our hope is Christ in the heart. —Matthew Henry
—Lloyd John Ogilvie[40]

WEEK 46

Silence   ❧   **Read**   ❧   **Reflect**   ❧   **Respond**   ❧   **Rest**

What words or phrases can you take with you from this experience to apply to your life today?

Jonah ran away from his calling. He went to Joppa and took a ship in the opposite direction. Tarshish could not have been further away from Nineveh. Jonah heard the call and got moving, but went in the wrong direction! He didn't say "No!" to the Lord—he just didn't go where the Lord told him. And yet the Lord intervened to get him back to where He wanted him. In Nineveh the people were very responsive to the petulant prophet. From the king down, the people repented.

Jonah ran from God and got into trouble; he ran with God and had great success: and finally he ran into the loving nature of God. The message of the book of Jonah is that we can keep our faith only when we give it away—even to people we don't like but who are infinitely loved by our Lord.

It is better to be in Nineveh with the Lord than in Tarshish without Him!
—*Lloyd John Ogilvie*[41]

WEEK 47

—

Passage: Philippians 4:10—13

Silence ❧ Read ❧ Reflect ❧ Respond ❧ Rest

What words or phrases can you take with you from this experience to apply to your life today?

Paul was in prison when he wrote these mood-modifying words. He was honest about the difficulties facing him but confident in the Lord's power to bring good out of painful circumstances. He was lifted out of the possibilities of a down mood by remembering the faithfulness of God in times past.

St. Richard of Chichester, a saint of the thirteenth century, penned a prayer which gives us a key to unlock the Lord's mood-changing power.

> *Day by day, dear Lord,*
> *Of Thee three things I pray:*
> *To see Thee more clearly,*
> *Love Thee more dearly,*
> *Follow Thee most nearly,*
> *Day by day.*

A change in my mood is but a prayer away.

—*Lloyd John Ogilvie*[42]

WEEK 48

Silence ❧ Read ❧ Reflect ❧ Respond ❧ Rest

What words or phrases can you take with you from this experience to apply to your life today?

Great things are promised, and they are imminent.
Incredible events are proclaimed, events that no human ear has heard;
Unveiled mysteries are opened up.
The earth and humankind are already quaking upon their advance.
And a prophetic voice cries into a frightened world;
The kingdom of heaven has come near.
The Lord God himself is coming, the Creator and Judge.
He comes with love for humankind.
He wants to take humanity home to the everlasting banquet.
He is coming.
Are you ready?
—Dietrich Bonhoeffer[43]

Silence   ❧   Read   ❧   Reflect   ❧   Respond   ❧   Rest

What words or phrases can you take with you from this experience to apply to your life today?

"Wonderful Counselor" (Is. 9:6) is the name of this child. In him the wonder of all wonders has taken place; the birth of the Savior-child has gone forth from God's eternal counsel.

"Mighty God" (Is. 9:6) is the name of this child. The child in the manger is none other than God himself. Nothing greater can be said: God became a child. In the Jesus child of Mary lives the Almighty God.

"Everlasting Father" (Is. 9:6) how can this be the name of the child? Only because in this child the everlasting fatherly love of God is revealed, and the child wants nothing other than to bring to earth the love of the Father. So the Son is one with the Father, and whoever sees the Son sees the Father.

"Prince of Peace" (Is. 9:6)—where God comes in love to human beings and unites with them, there peace is made between God and humankind and among people. Are you afraid of God's wrath? Then go to the child in the manger and receive there the peace of God.
—Dietrich Bonhoeffer[44]

Silence ❧ Read ❧ Reflect ❧ Respond ❧ Rest

What words or phrases can you take with you from this experience to apply to your life today?

God becomes human, really human. While we endeavor to grow out of our humanity, to leave our human nature behind us, God becomes human, and we must recognize that God wants us also to become human—really human. Whereas we distinguish between the godly and the godless, the good and the evil, the noble and the common, God loves real human beings without distinction. . . . God takes the side of real human beings and the real world against all their accusers. . . . But it's not enough to say that God takes care of human beings. This sentence rests on something infinitely deeper and more impenetrable, namely, that in the conception and birth of Jesus Christ, God took on humanity in bodily fashion. God raised his love for human beings above every reproach of falsehood and doubt and uncertainty by himself entering into the life of human beings as a human being, by bodily taking upon himself and bearing the nature, essence, guilt, and suffering of human beings. Out of love for human beings, God becomes a human being.
—Dietrich Bonhoeffer[45]

Silence   ❧   Read   ❧   Reflect   ❧   Respond   ❧   Rest

What words or phrases can you take with you from this experience to apply to your life today?

For the great and powerful of this world, there are only two places in which their courage fails them, of which they are afraid deep down in their souls, from which they shy away. These are the manger and the cross of Jesus Christ. No powerful person dares to approach the manger, and this even includes King Herod. For this is where thrones shake, the mighty fall, the prominent perish, because God is with the lowly. Here the rich come to nothing, because God is with the poor and hungry, but the rich and satisfied he sends away empty. Before Mary, the maid, before the manger of Christ, before God in lowliness, the powerful come to naught; they have no right, no hope; they are judged.

Who among us will celebrate Christmas correctly? Whoever finally lays down all power, all honor, all reputation, all vanity, all arrogance, all individualism beside the manger; whoever remains lowly and lets God alone be high; whoever looks at the child in the manger and sees the glory of God precisely in his lowliness.
—Dietrich Bonhoeffer[46]

Silence   ❧   Read   ❧   Reflect   ❧   Respond   ❧   Rest

What words or phrases can you take with you from this experience to apply to your life today?

None of us lives a life so rushed that it is impossible for us
to find even ten minutes a day, in the morning or evening,
when we can let everything around us become quiet
and submit ourselves completely to eternity,
when we can let it speak to us and ask it about ourselves.
In that way we can look very deeply within ourselves
and quite far beyond ourselves.
That might happen by looking at a few Bible verses or, even better,
by becoming utterly free and letting our soul make its way to the Father's house,
to its home, in which it will find rest.
—Dietrich Bonhoeffer[47]

ENDNOTES

THE WORD ON DWELL

1 Barry D. Jones, *Dwell: Life with God for the World* (Downers Grove, IL: InterVarsity Press, 2014), 96 of 3721 on Kindle.
2 Dictionary.com, s.v. "dwell," accessed August 27, 2025, https://www.dictionary.com/browse/dwell.
3 "Psalm 23:1–6," *Old Testament Parsing Guide, Vol. 2: Job–Malachi* (Chicago: Moody Press, 1990), 32.
4 J. I. Packer, *Knowing God* (Downers Grove, IL: InterVarsity Press, 1973), 53.

WHY 90 DAYS

1 N. T. Wright, *How God Became King: The Forgotten Story of the Gospels* (New York: 2011), 175.
2 Ralph Winter, "The Kingdom Strikes Back," *Perspectives on the World Christian Movement* (Littleton, CO: William Carey Publishing, 1991), 197–198.
3 Timothy Keller, *Center Church: Doing Balanced, Gospel-Centered Ministry in Your City* (Grand Rapids, MI: Zondervan, 2012), 13.

DWELL IN LECTIO DIVINA

1 "How Is it With Your Soul?" A Word with the Pastor, August 22, First United Methodist Church, accessed July 27, 2025, https://www.fumcpdx.org/about/news/august-really-mp8jn-62kh9-a3d6l.
2 Alice Fryling, *Seeking God Together* (Downers Grove, IL: InterVarsity Press, 2009), 66–68.

52 WEEKS OF LECTIO DIVINA

1 Eugene H. Peterson, *Reversed Thunder: The Revelation of John & the Praying Imagination* (New York: HarperCollins Publishers, 1988), 11.
2 Rueben P. Job and Norman Shawchuck, *A Guide to Prayer for All God's People* (Nashville: Upper Room Books, 1990), 67–68.
3 James Bryan Smith, *Hidden in Christ: Living as God's Beloved* (Downers Grove, IL: InterVarsity Press, 2013), 129.
4 Job and Shawchuck, *A Guide to Prayer for All God's People*, 80.
5 Ibid.
6 A. W. Tozer, *The Pursuit of God: The Human Thirst for the Divine* (Camp Hill, PA: Wing Spread Publishers, 1992), 36.
7 Job and Shawchuck, *A Guide to Prayer for All God's People*, 133.
8 Walter Wangerin Jr., *Reliving the Passion* (Grand Rapids, MI: Zondervan, 1992), 16.
9 Rueben P. Job, *A Guide to Spiritual Discernment* (Nashville: Upper Room Books, 1996), 95–96.
10 Wangerin, *Reliving the Passion*, 150.
11 Gordon T. Smith, *Called to Be Saints: An Invitation to Christian Maturity* (Downers Grove, IL: InterVarsity Press, 2014),129.
12 Ken Gire, *Reflections on the Word* (Colorado Springs: Chariot Victor Publishing, 1998), 30.
13 Henry T. Blackaby and Richard Blackaby, *Experiencing God Day by Day* (Nashville: B&H Publishing Group, 1998), 110.

14 Henri J. M. Nouwen, *Making All Things New: An Invitation to the Spiritual Life* (San Francisco: Harper & Row, 1981), 69.

15 Job and Shawchuck, *A Guide to Prayer for All God's People*, 230.

16 Blackaby and Blackaby, *Experiencing God Day by Day*, 279.

17 Job, *A Guide to Spiritual Discernment*, 95–96.

18 Ruth Haley Barton, *Sacred Rhythms: Arranging Our Lives for Spiritual Transformation* (Downers Grove, IL: InterVarsity Press, 2006), 28.

19 Richard Foster, *Celebration of Discipline: The Path to Spiritual Growth* (San Francisco: Harper & Row Publishers, Inc., 1978), 132–133.

20 Henri J. M. Nouwen, *A Cry for Mercy* (Garden City, NY: Double Day, 2002), 27.

21 Lloyd John Ogilvie, *God's Best for My Life* (Eugene, OR: Harvest House Publishers, 1981), 125.

22 Alice Fryling, *The Art of Spiritual Listening: Responding to God's Voice Amid the Noise of Life* (Colorado Springs: Shaw Books, 2003), 37.

23 J. I. Packer, *Concise Theology: A Guide to Historic Christian Beliefs* (Wheaton, IL: Tyndale House, 1993), 183.

24 Terry A. Smith, *The Lord Bless You* (Minneapolis: Chosen Books, 2023), 186.

25 Mac Pier, *A Disruptive God: Encounter Psalm 23 and Discover God's Purpose for You* (New York: Movement Day Publishing, 2018), 28–29.

26 Henri J.M. Nouwen, *The Selfless Way of Christ: Downward Mobility and the Spiritual Life* (Maryknoll, NY: Orbis Books, 2007), 70.

27 Ogilvie, *God's Best for My Life,* 324.

28 Ogilvie, *God's Best for My Life,* 356.

29 Mark Buchanan, *The Rest of God: Restoring Your Soul by Restoring Sabbath* (Nashville: W Publishing Group, 2006), 188.

30 Ogilvie, *God's Best for My Life,* 53.

31 Dietrich Bonhoeffer, *Wonder of Wonders: Christmas with Dietrich Bonhoeffer* (Louisville: Westminster John Knox Press, 2015), 45.

32 Ole Hallesby, *Prayer* (Minneapolis: Augsburg Publishing House, 1931), 36.

33 Peterson, *Reversed Thunder: The Revelation of John & the Praying Imagination* 59-60.

34 Job and Shawchuck, *A Guide to Prayer for All God's People* 143.

35 Peterson, *Reversed Thunder: The Revelation of John & the Praying Imagination*, 138.

36 Job and Shawchuck, *A Guide to Prayer for All Who Seek God,* (Nashville: Upper Room Books, 2006), 156.

37 Ogilvie, *God's Best for My Life*, 111.

38 Barton, *Sacred Rhythms: Arranging Our Lives for Spiritual Transformation*, 24.

39 Pier, *A Disruptive God: Encounter Psalm 23 and Discover God's Purpose for You*, 61.

40 Ogilvie, *God's Best for My Life*, 363.

41 Ibid., 325.

42 Ibid., 33.

43 Bonhoeffer, *Wonder of Wonders: Christmas with Dietrich Bonhoeffer*, 56.

44 Ibid., 44–46.

45 Dietrich Bonhoeffer, *God Is in the Manger: Reflections on Advent and Christmas* (Louisville: Westminster John Knox Press, 2010), 50.

46 Bonhoeffer, *God Is in the Manger: Reflections on Advent and Christmas,* 26.

47 Bonhoeffer, *Wonder of Wonders: Christmas with Dietrich Bonhoeffer*, 12.

ACKNOWLEDGMENTS

Marya and I want to acknowledge the tremendous editorial work of Charmain Sim. Charmain has assisted Movement.org with three book projects and two more on the way. We also want to thank Chloe Sng and her team for their fantastic design work.

David Sluka has been invaluable in working with the publishing of the book. Christy Distler has been our copyeditor on multiple projects.

Special thanks to our Movement.org board, Movement.org staff team, and the Global Advisory Team for your generosity of spirit.

Most importantly we give thanks to God, who has chosen to reveal Himself in His Word and in His Son.

ABOUT THE
AUTHORS

Dr. Mac Pier is the founder of Movement.org, and co-founded Movement Day with Tim Keller. He's served with InterVarsity Christian Fellowship, co-founded Concerts of Prayer and the Church Multiplication Alliance, and served the Lausanne Movement as Co-Catalyst for Cities. Mac earned his doctorate from Palmer Theological Seminary. He has authored/co-authored 10 books including *A Disruptive Gospel, A Disruptive Generosity, and A Disruptive God.* Mac and his wife Marya have lived in New York City for 40 years, and have three married children and six grandchildren.

Marya Pier is a former registered nurse and nurse practitioner, retired after 33 years of nursing in New York City where she has lived with her husband, Mac, for 40 years. She's mother to three married children and grandmother to six. She's a Bible Study Fellowship leader and has an Emmaus Certificate in Formational Leadership from Leadership Transformation, Inc.

www.ingramcontent.com/pod-product-compliance
Lightning Source LLC
LaVergne TN
LVHW051403080426
835508LV00022B/2950